My Story

AN AUTOBIOGRAPHY BY **ELVA HURST**

My Story

Printed in the United States of America
First Printing: October 2018
Second Printing: January 2023

ISBN 978-0-9786057-5-9

Cover design and layout by Josiah Hurst
www.josiahhurst.studio

DEDICATION

To my parents, who in love began my story.

CONTENTS

ABOUT THE AUTHOR

Self-taught artist and gifted author Elva Hurst draws inspiration from her warm memories of growing up in a large Old Order Mennonite family on a dairy farm in Lancaster County, Pennsylvania. Now with a husband, four children, and a small farm of her own, she carves time out of her busy day to follow her passion for the arts and writing—all from her kitchen table.

AUTHOR'S NOTE

This book was written for all you tourists who have visited Lancaster County and stopped by my Barnyard Art Studio and Gallery to see the chalk talk presentations. During your visits, you asked me a multitude of questions in your quest to learn more about the life and culture of the "plain people" of Pennsylvania.

You urged me to write my story, and I promised you that I would. I have always wanted to share my life experiences and the lessons I've learned with others to help them along their journey, but it just didn't seem like it was time yet. But finally, I feel like now is the time to share.

So, here it is... I trust many of your questions will be answered as you read. For me, it has been a positive experience to visit the past in my memory. In all the twists and turns of life, I was made aware again and again of the beautiful truths of Scripture. It says in Romans 8:28 that, "All things work together for good to those who love God, to those who are called according to his purpose," and in verse 37, "We are more than conquerors through him who loved us." Romans 8:39 encourages us with "... [nothing] else in all creation, will be able to separate us from the love of God that is in Christ Jesus our Lord."

Thank you for your interest in my story. I can only

hope that, in reading this book, your life will somehow be enriched and that you will be encouraged to be "more than a conqueror" in your situation.

May you discover your life's purpose and meaning as you live out your story.

God Bless,

IT'S NOTHING

fancy...

... SINCE I GREW UP

CHAPTER 1

Heritage and History

WHEN I WAS BORN IN 1968, MY FAMILY BELONGED TO THE OLD ORDER MENNONITE DENOMINATION, a sect of Mennonites similar to the Amish in that they still use horses and buggies for transportation.

I traced the beginnings of my German ancestors in Zürich Switzerland in the 1500s, during the time of the

Reformation. Religious leaders Conrad Grebel, Felix Manz, and others became disillusioned with the teachings of the state-run church. Believing their practices to be unscriptural, they rejected doctrines like infant baptism, believing that one should be baptized only upon the confession of faith as a responsible adult. These zealous young men baptized each other, making a break from the state church. The name "Anabaptists," meaning "re-baptizer," was given to them by their enemies. In the early days they called themselves "Brethren," but by 1545, during the leadership of Menno Simons, they came to be called "Mennonites." He too was troubled by the practices of the state church and left the Catholic priesthood to join the Anabaptist movement. Menno Simons became known as an evangelical preacher who believed that civil authorities had no right to control the church. He believed Christians should not take part in civil government, and that it was wrong to take any government position that involved violence of any form. Peace and love became a way of life. These non-conforming believers endured much injustice and suffered extreme persecution. Many were martyred as a result of their firm stand.

Despite severe persecution, great missionary zeal characterized the early Anabaptist movement, thus spreading quickly from Switzerland into Germany and Holland. During this difficult time of persecution, the leadership of Menno Simons saved the Dutch Anabaptists from succumbing to the many pressures placed upon them. In their fight for survival, however, they became legalistic in many of their practices.

A major concern of early Mennonites was to keep a pure church. Those who sinned fell under severe censure. The church excommunicated them if they did not repent; they were placed under the ban of communication. This practice brought serious disagreement. Some thought the banned person should be shunned in all social and economic relations, while others felt shunning should apply to spiritual fellowship and the communion table. Jacob Amman gained followers in his harsh interpretation of the ban and began a separate church body in the late 1600s. Amman wanted stricter enforcement of the ban while Hans Reist, their Mennonite Bishop, didn't agree with the interpretation. As a result of this difference, and other minor issues, Amman and his followers separated and became known as the Amish.

During the migration to America in the 1700s, Mennonites and Amish were drawn by William Penn who had sent representatives through Europe to invite all men to his province where religious freedom would prevail. Wearied by persecution and poverty, these peace-loving believers found refuge in Pennsylvania. Hundreds of Amish and Mennonites settled in southeastern Pennsylvania along streams and fertile valleys. Unhindered by civil government, they built their homes and families, practiced their faith, and enjoyed religious freedom. Lancaster County hosts the oldest and best-known Amish and Mennonite settlement today; however, there is a larger settlement further west in the state of Ohio.

I don't know at what age memory begins, but among my earliest memories are those of my grandparents. To me, they seemed very old. My maternal grandparents, David and Lizzie Burkholder, lived in a "Dawdy Haus" (Grandpa House) adjacent to Uncle Levi's farmhouse.

It's common practice today among the Old Order Amish and Mennonites for elderly parents not to go to nursing homes or retirement communities, but rather live nearby or with their children. I vividly remember the creaking windmill at the end of the walkway by the lane, and the pink pill-like candy my grandparents gave to me and my siblings every time we visited. I didn't like the candy because it reminded me of Pepto-Bismol, a pink medicine Mom made us swallow when we had an upset stomach. But I said "Danki" anyway because my Mother always admonished, "Elva, say thank you."

Grandpa Burkholder was a stern man. He liked to eat his eggs half raw because he felt they were healthier that way. My sickly grandmother, Lizzie, swallowed a whole egg raw as a daily tonic for her poor health!

Because of her poor health, she often stayed home from church. Instead, my Mom rode up front in the wagon seat with her dad. All the way to church Grandpa often moaned the blues about Grandma's poor health and medical bills and the farm bills. Consequently, at a young age Mom began to take the world on her shoulders.

Grandma Lizzie died when she was 86 years old. On my farm today, I named my brown-eyed Jersey cow in memory of my Grandma Lizzie.

My paternal grandparents; John and Katie Zimmerman lived closer to us so we visited more frequently. They lived on a quaint little farmette in the little village of Farmersville, PA. Like my other grandparents, they too had an old creaking windmill in the yard by the well shed. I liked to sit inside the shed just to listen to the sounds of the windmill.

Grandpa kept a few sheep in a small orchard pasture and a little red wagon in the outhouse nearby.

I played with the wagon and pretended I was the horse and the wagon was the carriage as I galloped around the backyard.

My father had a single sister named Nora who lived at home with Grandpa and Grandma. She and Grandma liked to cook and bake. They made all manner of cakes, pies, and other homemade sweet treats to serve us when we came to visit. Dad taught me to always put the toys away before we left and to shake hands "goodbye."

When we left for home, we went out through the screened-in front porch. By the door hung an old-fashioned embroidered sampler that read "Travel east; travel west after all home is best."

My only memory of my Grandparent's visit to our farm, before they passed, was during the grape harvest. Grandpa guided the horse and carriage through the front yard and pulled up close to the front door so my very heavy Grandmother did not have to walk as far. When she climbed down from the carriage it leaned dangerously to one side. I was afraid her weight would flip the carriage!

Once inside, Grandpa and Grandma sat face to face with a dishpan of grapes on a chair between them.

Together with my dad, they plucked the grapes from their stems while mom prepared to cook, process, and can the juice. They worked while they visited and caught up with the news around the home place.

This is my last memory of my grandparents; they died shortly thereafter. When Grandpa died, the clock on the mantel stopped ticking and his dog died too.

My father, Aaron Zimmerman, was the youngest of their six children. He grew up helping Grandpa around the farm. In those days everyone farmed with horses. Neighbors helped each other with harvest time work and other big events on the farm.

My father never forgot harvest time. He told me when He was nine years old, on the day before harvest, the steam engine was parked by the chicken house ready for harvest time work the next day. His father sternly told him, "Don't pull the whistle, it will scare the chickens."

My father was very curious about the massive machines bells, levers, and especially the whistle! Later that night my dad pulled the whistle but alas, the whistle got stuck! Thinking there was an emergency, the neighbors came running across the fields. My father panicked, ran for the house, and hid under his bed!

The whistle blew and blew for nearly an hour. The men tied a feed sack around it to muffle the ear-piercing sound. Finally, as a last resort, one of the men whacked it good with a hammer and the whistle stopped blowing! The night grew quiet again and the chickens returned to roost.

My mom's name is Eva. She was one of 13 children. She helped out on the farm too, riding the old draft horse named Jerry while he pulled the harrow over the fields to prepare them for planting.

One day, the horse had enough of the fieldwork and ran wildly for the barn. My mother lost her hold of the horse; tumbled down into the dirt and the harrow ran right over her. Thankfully, she survived the accident, suffering only from a slightly injured toe!

It was my mom's job to gather the eggs. She took her time and preached to the chickens in the hen house. In her pastime, Mom and her sisters would slide down the haystack, tuck their skirts into their bloomers, and climb the trees in the yard.

In their youth, my mom and dad ran around with the young folks in their church. Every weekend there was a singing held at someone's farm, after which they played a dancing game in the barn they called "stomping." My mom played old folk tunes like "She'll be comin' round the mountain when she comes..." on her harmonica to help the group step in time.

They played "Big Four" and "Wagon Wheel." Mom and Dad met while playing a "winking" game.

They were married several years later in 1952 and began a farm and family of their own.

Mom had four babies very close together; my two older sisters are only 14 months apart.

My dad insisted that she help him with the barn chores and fieldwork. She pumped water and heated it to do the washing; she baked bread, cooked three meals a day, and made homemade pies, cakes, and even crackers. Very few items were bought in the grocery store. It was not uncommon for farm women to work both in the house and the barn, but with Mom's unidentified health issues, it was hard for Dad to recognize she wasn't able to keep up the pace he expected. Mom worked herself to a frazzle and didn't get enough rest. Mom's health continued to decline. Weighed down by a guilty conscience from misbehavior during their dating days, and Dad's constant comparison of her to his sisters, she became discouraged and then depressed. Their marriage suffered from disrespect. Mom's emotional and mental health began to fail. Finally, the family took her to the mental institution for shock treatments. She dreaded them so fiercely that it only made matters worse. Twice she was committed.

Back home Shorty Shafer, a local hobo, came by the farm occasionally. In exchange for a night's sleep in the barn, he would help Dad with the fieldwork and then come to the house for a hot meal. He was aware of Mom's condition.

"How are you today, Eva," he inquired. It happened to be one of her "down days"; after a negative reply the hobo looked my mom straight in the eye and said firmly, "Eva, get ahold of yourself and tell the devil to get behind you!" My mom couldn't forget the hobo's words. Was this something she needed to resist? Was there a spiritual battle involved? From that day forward my mom began a journey back to health. Someone gave her a copy of *The Daily Bread*, a

Christian devotional that started coming to the house each month. With the entrance of God's Word, spiritual light and life came into her soul. She also remembered the words of advice she'd received from the institution: "Take care of yourself; no one else will" the doctor ordered.

She took time to rest and meditate on Scripture each and every afternoon. She learned how to implement healthy boundaries. She read the book the doctor had assigned to her and learned about health and nutrition. She began taking iron pills and B vitamins. Gradually her physical, mental, and emotional health returned.

Mom had five more children. I am her eighth child.

I was twelve years old when I overheard Mom relay her experience in a conversation between her and an older sibling. I was shocked to discover Mom had a nervous breakdown. I only saw my mother as being positive and peaceful; I could hardly believe what I had just heard. So complete was her victory that I saw no trace of her past struggles.

When Dad would fret, or we got tense and uptight, Mom would stay calm and say "Who trusts does not worry; who worries does not trust." She expressed faith through the many hymns and songs she sang as she worked.

Unfortunately, the memories of my father are not as pleasant. He was a task-oriented businessman and a very successful farmer. He owned several farms. He didn't deal well with life's stresses and took his frustrations out on those around him. Even so, I saw a tender side of him that would emerge from time to time, like on those days when it was raining and the hay was tucked away safe and dry in the barn, or he had a bowl of ice cream in front of him while opening up the milk check. My Dad loved to eat, especially sweets!

He had a serious sweet tooth. Food was his love language! On our way home from a visit to the relatives, as we approached the gas station, we began to chant from the backseat, "I scream, you scream we all scream for ice cream!" It always worked. Dad would grin, pull us to a stop, and buy us all ice cream sandwiches.

Dad fulfilled his role as a provider very well, but I was often left to feel like a nuisance as he constantly expressed his irritations and exasperations in an unhealthy way.

I wanted only to please my father, but we often felt tense around him since we never knew when he was going to "fly off the handle." Even so, thankfully the many good memories far outweigh the bad ones.

Years later a positive encounter would change Dad's personal life for the better.

CHAPTER 2

The Early Years

I WAS THE YOUNGEST IN OUR FAMILY UNTIL I WAS SIX YEARS OLD.

Since my siblings were in school, I played by myself. I preferred to play with cats rather than dolls. My siblings called me "the katza mammy," which means "the cat granny" in Pennsylvania Dutch. Perhaps I earned that nickname because our house cat, Missy, had a litter of kittens under the bed when I was born. Or, more likely, it was because I was often seen with a cat dangling from my arms. They would lay limp in my arms as I dropped milk into their mouths from a plastic doll bottle.

I roamed the fields and meadows of our farm; keenly remembering the sights and sounds of nature.

In the spring I searched for violets by the creek bank and picked buttercups in the meadow for my mom.

With no electronic distractions, I was attuned to my surroundings; I learned from nature. The farm pets were my playmates and the birds were my friends. I listened to their songs as I played by the creek bank.

We were very creative in our play. We transformed the wagon into a carriage with a large cardboard box. We cut out windows and doors, and then hand-sewed curtains for our "buggy" and painted the sides. My sister pulled the wagon as she played the part of the horse. We clip-clopped up and down our country road as I guided my "horse" with baler string.

One lazy warm summer afternoon, we decided to have a picnic in the walnut tree in the yard. We packed a lunch in a paper sack, hiked our skirts, and climbed the tree. All went well until we got into an argument. I got so upset with my sister that without thinking I gave her an angry push. To my horror she fell out of the tree and landed on her back, knocking the wind out of her. I was certain that I had killed my sister! In a panic, I ran for the house screaming for my mom. By the time Mom came out, my sister was back up on her feet, crying. I learned from that incident that it's best to control your temper.

My youngest brother was born the year I started school. Doc told mom "NO more children, it could kill you!" Nevertheless, Mom was 42 and child number nine was on its way. The cat ran down the stairs as the midwife hurried up. She fussed at the cat as she went. After the birth, we all gathered around her bed to discuss a name for the baby boy. Mom wanted her last child to be named after my father Aaron. My oldest brother, Paul, was 20 years old and owned his own silo-building business. He had a worker named Aaron and a friend named Ray. He suggested combining the two would make a good name. We all liked the sound of that, so it was decided-Aaron Ray would be his name.

I'm so glad Mother didn't listen to the Doctor's advice; I now had a younger brother and a playmate. He grew up and eventually took over the family farm. Often acting as a peacemaker, he is a great blessing to his siblings.

During my last winter at home with mom I grew bored, so while my siblings were at school Mom kept me occupied by having me cut out quilt patches. She cut a cardboard pattern from a cereal box that I then traced onto her scraps of material. She taught me how to cut the patches evenly and neatly, then sew them together by hand. I struggled with using the thread and needle; the thread often knotted up and I pricked my fingers. I did not care much for sewing, but still, it was fun to create what Mom intended to be a blanket for my doll. When it was finished I tried to wrap the cat in the blanket, but the cat did not appreciate it and ran off. So I lay on the floor behind Mom's old treadle sewing machine and ran the treadle for her as she sewed quilt tops. She would call out to me when to stop and start. It was especially exciting when she sewed me a new Sunday dress, which didn't happen very often because since I was the last of five girls I mostly wore hand-me-downs.

To pass the time I drew pictures of our farm on the pages of Mom's writing tablet. The lines bothered me but that was the only paper I had, so I tried to ignore them as I drew very primitive pictures of a barn and a house on a hillside with the sun rising in between. I drew a silo by the barn, a fence in the meadow, and birds in the sky. When it was finished, I'd tear it from the tablet and put it in the bottom drawer of Mom's sewing machine cabinet. Always the picture was the same; I drew it over and over again until the drawer was full. Today my favorite subject to paint is country farm scenes.

I was so happy when spring finally arrived. I skipped out to pick dandelions as mom cut the greens for salad and to brew for her health tea. I chased butterflies and grasshoppers and ran down to the garden to check the progress of the buds on the lilac bush. I could hardly wait until they bloomed.

One spring Sunday after lunch, Mom announced "Leave the dishes in the sink; we'll wash them later." Then we prepared for our annual spring outing by collecting as many vases and jars as we could find around the house, then piled them into the trunk of our neighbor Mrs. Siebert's car.

My mom didn't have a driver's license; she only knew how to drive a horse and buggy. So Mom, my sisters Ruth and Eva Mae, baby Aaron Ray, and I squeezed into the back seat of Mrs. Siebert's Honda along with her two children for a ride to the Old Siebert Place. We traveled a few miles over winding back country roads. Finally, we turned into a tree-lined farm lane. Slowly we made our way along the bumpy gravel surface.

Beyond the budding trees, the countryside was a colorful patchwork of fields, some plowed and browned, others splattered with golden dandelions and crimson clover.

Mrs. Siebert parked the car by the barnyard gate. Through the open gate, I saw before me a picture so wonderful I did not want to forget it. The Siebert's meadow, full of flowering bluebells, was a sea of violet, set against a cloudless soft blue sky the color of a robin's egg. Honeybees buzzed and butterflies danced, feasting on the sweet nectar of the tiny flowers that resembled little bells.

I reached down and pulled handful after handful of delicate little bells, held them to my nose, and inhaled their lavender-like fragrance. I reached for another then another. Together, we filled dozens and dozens of vases and jars till we grew tired and thirsty. "Come follow me!" called Mrs. Siebert. She led us to the edge of the meadow, down a narrow path beaten smooth by the shuffling of cattle's hooves. Cows are creatures of habit; they like to travel the same path to their favorite drinking spot. At home, our cows beat a path from the barn to the creek, from the creek to the shade tree, and back again to the barn.

We used these cows' paths as play roads for our tricycles and bicycles. Sometimes, we ran races on the paths in our bare feet, jumping cow pies as we went.

With our hands full of bluebells, we wound through a small grove of trees. As we entered the cool shade, my ears caught the sound of rippling water as it flowed from an old stone spring house, bubbling over pebbles and stones into a nearby creek.

As we neared the spring, I envisioned Ma in Laura Ingalls Wilder's book making her way to the spring where a panther stalked nearby. The spring I stood near was so similar to the description in the book, it gave me goosebumps and I began to feel fearful. My eyes scanned the trees for panthers stalking nearby.

"Oh stop it," I scolded myself, turning my attention to the little silver minnows in the water. Being careful not to muddy the water, we knelt down and cupped our hands to capture the cool, fresh spring water. The smells of the earth and the sight of the violets growing on the creek banks helped my fear fade away.

Mrs. Siebert filled the bucket with water. Then we followed her down the cow path back to the meadow, there we poured a little water into each vase to keep the bluebells fresh until we got home.

All too soon our bluebell outing was over. At home, we placed a bouquet of bluebells in every room of our farmhouse where they cheered the atmosphere with their delicate beauty. That evening I hurried with the barn chores. I couldn't wait to get back to the house to enjoy a book by the vase of bluebells in my bedroom.

* Mom picking bluebells with Aaron Ray

CHAPTER 3

School Days

"SEPTEMBER IS HERE, WITH ITS BRIGHT DAYS OF CHEER, AND WE ANSWER THE SCHOOL BELL'S GLAD CALL,"

Mother sang as she combed my long brown hair into braids. It was a bright September morning but cheer wasn't exactly what I was feeling. I felt a strange mix of excitement and worry. Would I like school? Would I miss Mom? Would the teacher be nice to me?

Worried questions troubled my mind as my siblings and I helped Mom pack our lunches. While we helped her make cold egg sandwiches, which I didn't care for very much, she told us that when she was a schoolgirl they often had molasses sandwiches and sometimes lard sandwiches packed in their lunches. Egg sandwiches didn't sound so bad after all. We added an apple, a jar of home-canned peaches, homemade cookies, and a thermos of raw chocolate milk. With lunch boxes in hand, we began our mile walk to our community's one-room school. I was thankful I did not have to walk alone. My sister Eva Mae was in the third grade. Ruth was in the fifth grade and Marvin was in the seventh grade. Earl had already finished school in the eighth grade. My teen sisters Vera and Alta worked in a nearby sewing factory, and my oldest brother Paul operated his used silo-building business.

My fears soon faded as I focused on the beauty of the morning. The bird's song in the woods, and the sound of the water as it rippled under the bridge while we crossed over, helped me to relax.

At the crossroad, our Amish neighbors, the Lapps, joined us in our walk to school. At the next road, another family joined us. Together we approached the small 19th-century-style one-room school. The school was called The Middle Creek School, named after the neighborhood creek nearby. It had been built by my father and other Mennonite neighbor men the year I was born in 1968. Dad donated our farmhouse bell to the new school.

The old iron bell on the rooftop had a pleasant calling sound to its ringing, just as Mother's song described that morning.

I visited the outhouse out back first before settling into a seat in the first row. Our classroom was very primitive. A globe sat on the corner of Teacher's desk, and a map of the world hung on the wall. The letters of the alphabet hung in a straight row above the chalkboard. In the back of the classroom extended a long shelf that held our lunch boxes, and in a corner shelf sat a large thermos with a small wash bowl beneath for hand washing at lunchtime. It was our job each morning to fill the thermos with water from the hand pump behind the schoolhouse. On the windowsill was the pencil sharpener. I soon discovered it was a nice break from lessons just to get permission to sharpen my pencil and have a brief look out the window.

After Teacher rang the small bell on her desk which we called "the second bell," we rose beside our desk to recite the Lord's Prayer together. Afterward, she lined us up as a choir in the front of the classroom. Sharing hymn books, we sang a few songs together. This quickly became one of my favorite times of the school day. I especially liked when she allowed us to pick the songs. Occasionally Noah Hurst, a local retired song leader from a Mennonite church, would stop by and give us a small lesson on music theory. He also taught us how to sing in four-part harmony. I discovered I could sing the alto parts. A few of the eighth-grade boys could sing bass and tenor. We enjoyed blending our voices together and heartily sang our favorite songs "Springtime in Glory," "Life's Railway to Heaven," "I'll Fly Away," and many other songs and hymns.

Back in our seats, we grew somber as Teacher pointed to the rules she had written on the blackboard mounted on the wall behind her desk:

1. *No whispering in class*
2. *No chewing gum*
3. *No cheating*
4. *No running in the classroom*

She also encouraged us to speak in English on the playground during recess time. We all spoke Pennsylvania Dutch at home and we needed to practice our English speaking skills.

I did not realize at the time how privileged I was to attend this private one-room school. History reveals a great struggle for the plain people to have gained the right and freedom to do so. In the early 1900s, new state guidelines for school consolidation included higher socially engineered education, progressive mandated subjects, longer school terms, and longer attendance, which Old Order Amish and Mennonite parents did not support. They believed that learning in such settings had little value and would threaten their way of life. They wanted formal schooling to remain basic and in harmony with the goals of the church and home. They believed that vocational skills and life science were learned best on the farm or in the family trade, and they felt these changes were not compatible with that ideal.

Amish families resisted sending their teens beyond the eighth grade which resulted in many arrests, fines, and in some cases, even imprisonment. In Buchanan County, Iowa, authorities took action to close the Amish private school. On one school morning in November, officials arrived to forcibly bus the children to town. The children walked obediently towards the bus until an Amish father yelled "Run!" in German and the children dashed for the surrounding cornfields. The press caught images of fleeing children and angry officials. The next week public education officials arrived at the school once again. This time the children did not run; instead, they loudly sang "Jesus Loves Me." Mothers cried and stern-faced fathers stood in the doorway. National sympathy began to form toward the Amish. Private contributions poured in to help pay the fines and penalties.

A legal battle erupted in Pennsylvania in the mid-1930s when Lancaster County school districts began closing rural one-room schools and busing children out of their communities to larger public school buildings. This resulted in Amish protests that also drew media attention. Some Amish and a few non-Amish friends hired lawyers from Philadelphia. Church leaders petitioned legislators with a 130-foot-long letter containing some 3,000 Amish and Mennonite signatures that was sent to the state capital in Harrisburg. An Amish committee known as the Delegation for Common Sense Schooling met with legislators to reach a compromise.

During the 1937-1938 school year, two private elementary schools opened in Lancaster County, marking the beginning of a new era of parochial education. By the end of the school year, legislature also reduced the compulsory attendance age from sixteen to the age of fourteen. The plain people had successfully fought and won the legal right to establish and operate their own schools, or to withdraw from public schools after completing the eighth grade!

As remarkable as this story is, I was not a very grateful beneficiary of my forefathers' values and courage. I decided I didn't like being in school. I missed my farm pets too much!

In our one-room school we never addressed our teacher as Miss or Mrs.; that felt too fancy to us. We always only called her "Teacher."

Our studies began with arithmetic, which I quickly discovered I disliked very much, nor did I enjoy vocabulary or English. Spelling, reading, and history went much better for me. We had no science class, but Teacher did make time for art during the last period on the last day of the week. All week I looked forward to this time for art, even though she rarely taught us art, but only gave us pictures in keeping with the season of the year to color neatly. Then she would mount them on colored construction paper and decorate the school walls with our pictures.

Occasionally she would announce "Today we are going to do freehand drawing."

Everyone groaned and so did I because I wanted to blend in when secretly I was pleased to have this chance to draw!

After studies were finished, and as we waited on Teacher to finish a subject with another class, we were allowed to read a library book. Our library consisted of a bookcase with five shelves. The lower level held the picture books and early readers such as the *Bobbsey Twins* and the *Little House on the Prairie* books. I quickly discovered I loved to read. As I moved on up the grades, I read all the *Nancy Drew* mystery books and traded *Zane Grey* and *Hardy Boys* books with the boys in my class. Since we had so few books, I read and reread the same books many times over!

During our elementary years in school, we had a tradition of taking brand-new coloring books to school and inviting our classmates to color in them. We would pick a page and color it as neatly as possible, then sign our name, always trying to outdo one another. Once, I brought a new coloring book. I proudly passed it around but I did not invite the Amish girl, Sarah, to color in my book. I did not like her very much. I was mostly jealous of her since she often had store-bought goodies in her lunch box such as Twinkies and candy bars. We never had goodies from the store in our lunches because we believed it was frivolous to buy something when you could make it, so it was even more painful when she gloated about her goodies. I saw a chance for revenge and did not pass the coloring book to her. This hurt her feelings so much that during class she put her head down in her arms and sobbed loud and long, disrupting the entire school from their studies. The feeling of vindication was very brief. Teacher marched to her desk and demanded to know what happened. Between broken sobs, Sarah told it all...

"Elva.... won't (sob) let...me color (sob, sniff...) in her coloring book!"

With her hands on her hips, Teacher whirled around to face me and exclaimed, "Elva, I'm surprised at you, I can't believe you would do such a thing!"

She insisted right then and there that I give my coloring

book to Sarah to color a page. Obediently I handed the coloring book to Sarah, she wiped her tears and our studies resumed.

But that was not the end of the incident. That evening, as I was setting the table for supper, I saw Sarah's Mom come marching down the road. Right on past the house she went; she was headed straight for the barn to talk to my Dad! Instantly I lost my appetite as I awaited more punishment, but to my surprise, at milking time Dad only scolded me. "Now you be nice to Sarah, make sure I don't ever hear anything like that again!" As for Sarah and I, our relationship mended with time. We still keep in touch today even though she lives in the far-off state of Kansas. She comes to see me whenever she visits Pennsylvania.

My favorite part of the school day was the nature walk home from school. Very often I took the shortcut through the field down along the meadow fence. I walked by the creek just to hear the song of the stream as the water rippled and gurgled around the rocks by the creek bank. The walk led me on through the edge of the woods. As I entered, I left the day's trouble behind and inhaled the rich scent of the woods. Eagerly I looked for signs of the changing seasons. In the spring I searched for violets by the creek bank. In the fall I collected colorful leaves and paused to watch them float on down the stream. In the wintertime, I noticed the footprints of the wildlife in the snow, and watched as a cardinal flew by on bright wings of beauty. I sighed and wished for a moment that I could be like that bird: carefree, with no tests, no new teachers, and no school bully to worry about. I couldn't linger long though; there were chores to be done at home.

I exited the woods at the road and crossed over the bridge. I paused to consider a temptation: the arithmetic test with a failing grade was still in my pocket. Teacher wanted me to show it to my parents.

"No one will ever find out." I reasoned.

I drew the paper from my pocket, then threw it over the railing of the bridge into the water. I ran to the other side of the bridge to watch it float down the stream! I was wrong of course. I knew about it, and now my conscience bothered me and poor tests always showed up on the report card. Eventually, my parents would find out about it anyway.

I began to carry both the weight of a guilty conscience and the dread of arithmetic. Teacher never assigned homework. We were all from farm families and there was too much work to be done at home; no one had time for schoolwork, but one day in the fourth grade I brought my assignment home to see if Mom could help me understand fractions. She was too busy making supper.

"Go ask Pop." She said as she stirred the soup.

Dad sat waiting for supper in the nearby kitchen rocking

chair reading the Lancaster Farming Newspaper. Timidly, I approached him with the arithmetic textbook in my hand and asked him to explain it to me.

"Humph." He grunted and set aside his newspaper.

He proceeded to quickly, gruffly explain the lesson. I tensed when I told him, "I'm still not sure what you mean." Dad turned to me, raised his voice, and angrily declared "Die bich an dumie!" ("You are a dummy!" in Pennsylvania Dutch).

Dad's words went deep inside my being and stayed there to haunt me for years. Whenever I came up against a new concept in school I heard those words repeated back to me: "You are a dummy."

Unfortunately, Dad called me that too many times, and I believed those careless words. They became truth to me. I agreed with them, often thinking to myself "I can't, because I'm a dummy."

As my grades declined so did my self-esteem.

However, not all of my days in school were unpleasant. The good memories of my elementary years are still very precious to me.

Occasionally Teacher would announce a lunch box exchange for the next day. We all put our names in a hat. The next day we were to pack a nice lunch all by ourselves for the person whose name we picked. I picked the name of a boy that I liked. All during milking time that evening I planned what kind of special lunch I would pack for him.

I baked a batch of chocolate chip cookies after milking. The next morning, I added a jar of home-canned applesauce with an added dash of cinnamon. Then I made a peanut butter and jelly sandwich. For a special treat, I spread peanut butter between soda crackers then hurried off to school.

At noon we quietly sat at our desks and waited as one by one, students placed their lunches on the desk of the person whose name they had picked. Eli approached my desk with his black tin boy's lunch box in his hand and a wide grin on his face. I suddenly felt suspicious since Eli was known for his pranks. I carefully inspected the food he had packed before I ate it. I opened the baloney sandwich and checked between the layers of lettuce and cheese to make sure he didn't put any earthworms in the sandwich. I was delighted to find a bag of chips and a giant-sized chocolate whoopie pie in the lunch box, which I saved for last. Slowly I licked the soft gooey icing, listening to the happy sounds of classmates as they showed off the special treats they had found in their lunches.

Maybe school wouldn't be so bad after all...

* My class picture (grades 1-8)

* The same school I grew up in, present day

CHAPTER 4

Three Difficult Years

THE MIDDLE CREEK SCHOOL WAS GETTING TOO CROWDED TO HOLD ALL EIGHT GRADES,

so the school board decided to send the fourth and fifth grades, transported by van, to Millport School (an Amish school in another district nearby).

I was entering the fourth grade that year, and not only did I find book learning very unpleasant, but fragile self-esteem and fear of new classmates were added to the mix.

In the new school, the boys were loud and rowdy and dirty-minded. The teacher was timid. She quickly lost control of the classroom. I often saw her dissolve into tears behind the row of books on her desk. The chaos made it nearly impossible for me to concentrate on my lessons. At recess time I silently withdrew, trying to avoid the boys but, as it is with human nature, I became an easy target for their teasing. I did not know how to stand up for myself.

They teased me mercilessly. When I walked through the hallway I was ambushed by the boys. They ripped my blue Mennonite coat off of me then they took turns to wear it (they were only allowed to wear black coats), and chanted "Look at me, I'm English, I'm English."

I soon realized "the English" is what the Amish called anyone outside their circle, even though I could barely speak English myself.

Every day I woke up with a stomach ache. I didn't tell Mom at first, but eventually she noticed something was wrong. She offered me a cup of freshly brewed peppermint tea. I don't know which helped me the most, the tea or her loving gesture. Nevertheless, off to school I went, facing another dreaded school day.

Wintertime came, and so did the snow. On snowy days I avoided the outdoors for fear of the boys' snowball attacks. I avoided the necessary trips to the outhouse, waiting instead for the end of the day and the time to go home; which resulted in frequent urinary tract infections. One day during recess I just couldn't put it off any longer. Without my coat, I quickly slipped through the back door, then ran as fast as I could. Suddenly, three boys ambushed me from behind, pushed me down into the snow, and shoved snowballs into my underwear. I was stunned. I stumbled to my feet with tears blinding my eyes as I ran for the refuge of the outhouse. Inside, I heard their voices surrounding the outhouse. I was too afraid to return to the schoolhouse so I waited and waited, shivering in the cold. After a while, I heard the bell ringing, but still I waited to be sure the boys had gone inside.

When I returned to the classroom I was mortified to realize I had missed the second bell. I swallowed really hard as Teacher scolded me for being tardy.

Eagerly I looked forward to the second and final year at Millport School. I looked forward to the change back to Middle Creek School where everything would be alright again. It was then that we got word that my class would stay at Millport for a third year until the sixth grade. I couldn't stand the thought of staying at Millport School. I went to Mom in tears, begging her to send me somewhere else. Mom expressed her concern to Dad. For a brief moment, I saw understanding in Dad's eyes. He and Mom discussed other options. "Well, she could go to Wood Corner School. But ach no, that's too far away." Dad reasoned.

"How would she get there? The bus doesn't come this far.

Besides, I can't drive her there every day." Then he turned to me.

"No, you'll just have to stick it out at Millport School. You can make it," He added. "It's just one more year."

I began to lose my appetite. As the days drug on I began to suffer indigestion. I considered coping strategies such as "stay away from the Amish boys" or "maybe I could get sick more often; then I could stay at home." I noticed they didn't pick on the other Mennonite girl in my class. In fact, they rarely ever teased her. If they did, she would go toe to toe with them and threaten to punch them in the nose.

I just didn't have the courage to do that until one day, the unthinkable happened. Teacher was preoccupied with helping the eighth-grade class at the opposite end of the classroom. The boy in the seat in front of me pulled a jump rope from his desk, turned to me with a wicked grin on his face, and suddenly the rope was tightly wrapped around my upper body. I couldn't protect myself since, at the same time, the boy behind me tied my hands behind my back. Another boy across the aisle was pulling my dress up through the ropes. When I realized that their mission was to see my underwear, something rose up inside of me. I yanked hard and tried to pull myself free. All the while, up, up, up went my dress. Just then a girl reached across the other aisle with scissors and cut the rope. I unwound the rope, but the boy behind me tried again to tie me up. I grabbed my pencil, whirled around, and stabbed the boy behind me in the arm with the pencil's point. By then, Teacher came scurrying to our end of the room to investigate the commotion.

Once more she scolded me for being out of my desk but this time I didn't care. She did nothing about the incident.

Even so, I felt as though I had won a battle. The boy behind me was clutching his arm, muttering something about the pencil lead causing blood poisoning. "I don't care about that either! Serves him right," I thought.

Strangely enough, something inside me shifted. I still didn't enjoy Millport School, and I was counting down the days until the first week of May and the last day of school, but I wasn't as afraid of the boys anymore. They never tried any mischief on me after that incident; they only teased from a distance!

* *Middle Creek School on a cloudy day*

CHAPTER 5

Angel in Disguise

HER LARGE FRAME FILLED THE DOORWAY OF THE SCHOOLHOUSE AS SHE RANG THE BELL TO CALL US INSIDE.

She wore a large, solid white head covering tied tightly under her multiple chins. She was tough, firm, and kind all at the same time. Her heart was as large as her frame.

Her name was Anna Hurst. She had a reputation among the plain schools... "She can straighten out any school!" I heard the adults say about her. Apparently, Middle Creek

School needed some changes too. Not only did she bring change to the whole class dynamic, but to my personal life as well.

She was older and wiser than my previous teenage teachers. Immediately she brought law and order to the classroom. She walked among the desks as she taught. She carried a ruler in her hand and she wasn't afraid to use it. Once, during morning devotions, I was absentmindedly fiddling with the pencils on my desk. The next thing I knew, my knuckles were burning! The whole room got quiet; no one dared to make any noise as she taught.

At recess time she walked among the playground to make sure we were playing fairly and that no nonsense was going on in the back corner of the playground. She made us all play together and didn't allow cliques to form among us. She also taught us some new, fun games. She was too heavy to run so she shouted out instructions from the edge of the ball field.

I can still see her with her hands on her hips, shielding her eyes from the sun. When she was satisfied that things were under control, she returned to her desk to grade papers. Once, I returned to the classroom to get my sweater just in time to catch her reaching for something in the bottom drawer of her desk. She acted as though she didn't want me to see it. That made me even more curious. Later, when she went to the outhouse, I peeked into the drawer. It was full of king-sized Snickers bars! I quickly closed the drawer resisting the urge to steal one. Snickers bars were my favorite candy too! So that is how she coped. Perhaps that is one reason why she was so heavy, I reasoned!

She was a Spirit-filled Christian who had a spiritual sense about her. A decrement that helped her get to the root of any issue rather quickly.

She immediately noticed my struggle with arithmetic. After explaining the new concepts to the class, she would call me aside to her desk to explain the lesson to me in a way I could understand. At first, I was embarrassed about that, but I grew to appreciate it. She understood my learning style.

I've heard it said that "A good teacher makes difficult things easy."

That was our teacher Anna Hurst. She also detected my bad attitude about learning, which was rooted in the bad things I believed about myself. When I complained that I couldn't understand, she got into my face and said "Yes, you can do it!" I soon realized I could learn. I was not a dummy after all. I could learn! With peace and quiet restored in the classroom, I could concentrate much better on my lessons. My report card began to reflect much better grades. My heart was thrilled to see A's and B's instead of D's and F's! I proudly showed them off to Mom and Dad. "Oh, that's good!"

Mom praised. Dad just grunted, but I knew he was pleased.

I loved how spontaneous Teacher could be. She often rewarded us with an extra recess or brought us treats from home. We could be in the middle of a history lesson, then she would suddenly break into a giggle at a funny memory. I never forgot how animated she became when she told us how she was helping her husband bring hay down from the hayloft for the cows one evening when suddenly, her husband began to prance and dance around and around, slapping his knees and thighs as he went. Finally, he released the buckle of his overalls and dropped his pants and a mouse scurried off into the hay! We erupted in fits of laughter and laughed so hard we cried! At other times she grew serious as she told us true stories of people's poor choices and the resulting consequences. Her lessons for life were rather "caught" than "taught."

On rainy days we played fun learning games indoors. I didn't like to spell, but when we played spelling baseball, I was suddenly interested. The players were stationed at bases in the four corners of the classroom. Teacher was the pitcher and "threw" out the word for the batter to spell. If correct, he could go to first base and the next player stepped up to the plate. And so, pleasantly, the rainy day passed rather quickly.

Teacher Anna belonged to an Old Order conservative

Dunkard Brethren Church that was still very plain in lifestyle, but they allowed cars for transportation instead of buggies. Anna Hurst had a large cargo van with no seats in the back. We sat along the edge of the floor; we were cramped but very happy for the adventure as she drove the upper graders to various educational field trips. And always she would stop for ice cream on the way home. As she drove, she put in cassette tapes of gospel songs and hymns. I loved music and listened intently as she drove. The words of the gospel songs sowed good things in my heart and lifted my spirit.

Slowly but surely my soul was being restored. I no longer dreaded going to school. Instead, on school mornings I was excited about the day ahead. My last and final year in the eighth grade went by in a happy blur with many new discoveries and much better grades.

* My cousins and I in 8th grade

CHAPTER 6

A Discovery

TODAY I STILL BENEFIT FROM THE MANY POSITIVE THINGS TEACHER ANNA HURST SOWED INTO MY LIFE.

Unbeknownst to me at the time, she rerouted my whole life and set me on a positive course for a lifetime. Not only did she understand my learning style, thus salvaging my education, but she also noticed I liked to draw. She drew out my interest in art. She provided me with many new art experiences. Previously, I had very little exposure to art. I can honestly say as a child I never met another artist.

I did not realize I was destined to be an artist; I only

knew I liked to draw. I eagerly looked forward to the last period of the school day on Friday, the time set aside for art.

Teacher brought her leftover tubes of fabric paint which we used to color in our drawings. She also brought watercolors to school. With them, we painted colorful designs on paper dollies, then mounted them on construction paper and taped them on the wall. She taught us how to shade and blend with colored pencils. I was in my glory! She gave me the foundation I would need to build on the art form I would soon discover.

Recently, Anna Hurst passed away at age 96. It seems as though her longevity was not hindered by those king-sized Snickers bars she loved so much! She had a zest for life. She loved life and life loved her back.

Shortly before her passing, I was able to visit her. I took with me my early school days paintings, then showed her some of my recent works. She was so happy to see me. Her mind was keenly alert. She took in every detail of our visit. In our parting handshake she pointed upward and instructed me one last time, "Now, you stay close to Him." She said.

Throughout my upper-grade school days, and during the summertime, I was often hired out to work on my oldest brother's farm in Berks County, PA. I was 11 years old when I was first hired out and very homesick! I worked hard in the garden, mowed the yard, and helped my brother unload hay bales. I helped to milk cows each morning and evening.

I looked forward to an hour of reading at bedtime. In those summers I learned how to cook for a family and take care of babies. Whenever a new baby was born to my older siblings' families, I was called on to help out.

In the summer of 1978 I was sent to my sister Vera's house to help out with her newborn who was born with a heart defect and needed much care. I helped out by holding baby Charlene and rocking her often. I helped my sister keep up with the garden and housework. Eight months later baby Charlene died.

I watched as the tiny little coffin was placed into the ground. Trying not to cry, I focused instead on the miracle of a new body for baby Charlene in Heaven. I continued to stay at Vera's house. I watched her process her grief. She began to paint pictures. I sat at her kitchen table and watched her paint. My hands longed to hold the brush. That summer she did not pay me in dollars for the help I had given her. Instead, she paid me with things a teenager might need. She bought me my first wristwatch. It was the only piece of jewelry I was allowed to wear. Vera also taught me how to use underarm deodorant and how to neatly fix my hair under my prayer covering. It was tradition in our Mennonite church when girls turned 14 to put up their hair in a bun and begin to wear prayer coverings. For me, this was something of a passage from childhood to adulthood. Some days I was glad and felt grown up. On other days I still wanted to run and play. It was those days that I missed my pigtails!

One day, my sister paid me with a set of enamel paints and brushes. She took me to visit Edna Sauder, an Old Order Mennonite artist. I sat on the sofa and watched her paint. I watched how she mixed the paint on her brushes, then blended shadows and highlights. I couldn't wait to get home and try my hand at painting.

As soon as I was finished with the barn chores, I looked for a flat stone in the field. I also found some old roof slate in Dad's barn. When I tried to paint on my own it was not nearly as easy as it looked.

This was not the first time I tried to paint. One summer, when I was eleven, I found Testors enamel model paints in my brother's garage and baby food jars in mom's attic. The paint didn't stick well to the glass. I grew frustrated and gave up. Next time, I was determined to make it work. I tried so hard that I got headaches every time I painted. Mom took me to see a Mennonite reflexologist. The treatments helped to relieve the tension headaches.

Eventually, when I learned to relax and be more graceful with myself, things went much better. Throughout my teen years, I continued to self-educate in art by studying art books I had collected from thrift stores and garage sales. I followed the advice in these old books to practice often. I read it takes three things to be a good artist:

1. Practice
2. Practice
3. Practice

So, I made myself practice painting every day, even on those days when I didn't feel like painting. Very quickly my skills improved, and that encouraged me to keep on painting! At first, Mom and Dad did not appreciate all the time I spent painting, but when they saw it was more than a passing phase, they began to take notice of my work.

The Mennonite artist sent my way an art dealer named Wilbur Graybill from Juanita County.

I was very nervous when he came to our farm in his big white truck. He opened that back door and showed me stacks of saws and cast iron skillets. My Dad helped me carry the things to the house. He seemed pleased with the prospect of this business venture. The dealer left me a stack of things to paint instructing me to paint Lancaster county farm scenes, covered bridges, and grist mills. I soon settled into a comfortable routine of milking cows with dad and painting during the day. I was only fourteen and a half years old and already I had my first full-time art job!

Throughout my teen years, the art dealer came regularly. He would suggest I add a tractor to the barn scene or put cows and horses in the pasture. Thus, my art compositions improved. Dad's interest in my art grew as well. He would look over my shoulder where I painted at Mom's kitchen table and comment, "I like the deer you painted."

I was puzzled as I had not painted a deer in the scene. "I didn't paint a deer," I replied.

"Oh, you can't see him, he's behind the tree!" Dad replied laughingly.

I realized that with my artwork I had gained Dad's attention and approval. This spurred me to paint even more. Some evenings I would stay up late into the night to finish a project. I continued this habit until one night Dad gave me a stern but caring lecture, saying, "Nighttime is for sleeping. Get yourself to bed!"

When Sunday guests would come to visit, Dad took them to the back shanty where I kept my painted items that were ready for the dealer to pick up. The visitors would comment on the scenes as Dad proudly held up large crosscut saws and milk cans that I had painted. They would ask my dad "Where did your girl get this talent? From you Aaron?"

"Why no, not from me," Dad quipped "I still got my talent."

"Prove it Pop!" I thought to myself.

Decades later, after his passing, I found some simple

sketches on pieces of cardboard tucked between stacks of Dad's farming newspapers. Today I proudly display them for visitors who come to visit my studio and gallery from around the nation.

I was sixteen years old when I signed up to attend a local art and craft show in the nearby town of Ephrata. I was quite nervous about this new experience and afraid of the thought of talking to strangers. I prepared lots of hand-painted items. I painted pictures on pieces of broken roof slate, crocks, tin cups, cast iron skillets, and such. The night before the art show, I had trouble falling asleep. I was both excited and anxious at the same time.

I didn't have a driver's license yet, so I piled the merchandise, a table, a chair, and a money box in my sister Ruth's car. She drove me to the show, helped me set up, and then left. The show opened and the crowds began drifting by my display, pausing to comment on the artwork. I trembled in my chair, feeling very bashful. To my surprise, they began to purchase and did not stop! My table was nearly bare when Ruth came to pick me up. I was so pleased with the outcome of the show. It felt so good to have faced up to my fear of people and business.

I realized this new venture wasn't nearly as bad as I had feared.

In those early years of business, I discovered no matter

how poorly my paintings were, in those days, if I painted a horse and buggy in the scene, it sold! I catered to the interests of the tourists that came to visit Lancaster County, which became one of the secrets to my artistic success.

I also discovered a specialty art in painting farm scenes on old milk cans. Farmers would bring me pictures of their farms to be painted as a gift to the family, presenting a picture of the home farm on the milk can.

Painting country farm scenes quickly became my favorite subject.

Since formal art training was out of the picture, I learned wherever and from whomever I could. We had no internet or free online tutorials in those days, so I signed up for a class called Painting in Pastels at a local art supply store. I discovered I enjoyed painting with soft pastels. I liked that there was no need for brushes or water. I enjoyed using my fingers to mix and blend colors. However, I only participated for three class sessions. We felt the price of the class was too expensive. I continued to practice the technique on my own, still mostly painting primitive pictures with enamel paints on old items.

Edna Sauder invited Vera and me to her house for monthly gatherings we called "painting parties." I eagerly looked forward to meeting with other Amish and Mennonite artists. We would arrive in the morning and set up our paints at her long farmhouse kitchen table. We chatted as we painted and shared new ideas and art inspirations. Then at lunchtime, we shared a covered dish meal; each artist would bring her favorite dish to share. Emma Zook, the Amish artist, always brought her warm iced homemade sticky buns, freshly baked just that morning! We painted the afternoon away until it was time to go home and prepare supper for our families.

The only other instructional class I can remember as a teen happened when I was 17 years old. While visiting the shopping mall with my girlfriends on a Saturday night, we met an artist painting portraits with chalk pastels. I was fascinated by how quickly he worked. I stood and watched him paint while the other girls shopped. He urged me to sit down to have my portrait painted for only $25. I gave him a picture of my boyfriend and he painted a picture of him too. I felt as though I had splurged but I was very pleased with the portraits. I took them home, had them framed, and hung them in my bedroom. The artist invited me to attend a class at his studio in the city of Harrisburg.

I was working for my sister Vera at the time, so her husband agreed to drive me and my artist friend to the painter's studio. It was a stressful drive to the city during rush hour traffic. We drove around and around the block till we finally found the address. This being one of my first experiences in the city, I decided then and there that I would not like city life. I held tightly to my purse and sketchbook, as I had heard there were lots of pickpockets in the city.

We entered the large building and started up a long, grand, winding staircase. At the top of the landing stood a nude statue. I blushed and tried not to look at it. We went to the third floor where the artist greeted us warmly and welcomed us inside. The room was crowded with busy advanced-level artists at their easels. Mr. Gilroy guided us to the front and announced that "Tonight we will draw portraits in pencil."

I placed my large sketchbook on an easel and took a deep breath. I had never drawn from a live model before, and I was very nervous.

Mr. Gilroy asked my brother-in-law to pose as our model. Allen sat, quiet and still, in a chair under a spotlight. Everyone but me began to draw. I was overwhelmed. I didn't know where to begin. Mr. Gilroy, noticing I was having trouble, came over to my easel and kindly guided my steps.

Finally, we were finished. I was relieved that the class was over. Mr. Gilroy took our money and invited us to join next week's class. The subject was to be a live nude figure drawing. We quickly left, hurrying past the nude statue out front. Returning was out of the question; I was not willing to compromise my purity of heart and mind in the name of art!

My studio in the back shanty

The first acrylic on slate painting I ever attempted

CHAPTER 7

A Greater Discovery

THROUGHOUT MY CHILDHOOD AND PRE-TEEN YEARS, I SUFFERED BOUTS OF ANXIETY AND INSECURITY.

I couldn't look another person in the eye. I suffered from crippling insecurity and feared everything from spiders in our cellar, to thunderstorms, and even motorcycles on the road! When I was little, my older brother told me that the men in the dark clothes on those loud motorcycles were part of the Hell's Angels motorcycle gang; we figured every motorcycle and its rider were bad. On our walk to and from school, whenever we heard their loud motors in the distance, we made a beeline for the corn field and hid among the rows of corn. With hearts pounding, we waited until the "Hells Angels" passed.

It's somewhat of a mystery that I experienced so much fear and insecurity when I was sheltered from so much. I never saw a broken home, drugs or alcohol abuse; I never read the daily paper or saw the evening news! We had no TV in our homes, no violent video games, and still, I had fear—lots of fear.

Today, I realize no matter our creed or cultural background, the enemy of our souls tries to find a way to destroy us all. The Bible says in John 10:9 that Satan comes to "Kill, steal, and destroy..." Since this problem is of a spiritual origin, it must be remedied spiritually. I discovered the missing dimension when I entered into a personal relationship with God.

Before that time, I had an awareness of God but He seemed distant and far away.

I never heard the salvation message preached clearly in our Old Order Mennonite church. Thankfully, I was a reader. I liked to read true stories, particularly biographies and autobiographies. I'll never forget when I read a novel called *Lucy Winchester*. It was a very sad story of a difficult life. I shed tears over the book and, at the end, when I discovered it was not a true story, it made me so angry. "You mean I wasted tears on a fake story?" I thought to myself. Needless to say, I lost my taste for fiction!

Instead, I read books like *The Hiding Place*; the story of Corrie Ten Boom, the Dutch heroine who risked her life to hide the Jews during Nazi Germany. Her family suffered in the horrors of the concentration camps where her sister Betsy and her father both died, but Corrie survived. Later, she traveled the world with a message that went like this: "There is no pit so deep, that God's love isn't deeper still."

I marveled at Corrie Ten Boom's faith and courage, and the power of forgiveness and being forgiven.

In another true story, I read about the author's experience of "accepting Christ as your personal Savior" and what it meant to be "born again." That was a new term for me. I began to read the New Testament for myself. In so doing, I discovered a verse in the book of Acts that stated, "Believe on the Lord Jesus Christ and you shall be saved."

What did it mean to "believe" and be "saved"?

Did it really mean to only believe?

I was very aware of sin and sin's destructions, but I did not understand salvation's solution.

In my readings, I became aware that the cross is a place of substitution. He did it for me; Christ died for my sins. One night, in the quiet privacy of my bedroom, I prayed to receive Jesus. It was a simple, but heartfelt prayer. I've heard it said, "the perfect prayer is the one you mean with all your heart." After the prayer, I felt a deep inner peace and a knowing that when I died I would go to Heaven.

As wonderful as that salvation experience was, my mind, will, and emotions were still a mess and needed "saving" too. I still worried, feared, and was anxious about the future.

I also had a sense there was more...that is when, quite by accident (or shall we say "by the providence of God"), I picked up a ministry magazine called the *Word of Faith* I saw lying on the kitchen table. I was not particularly interested in its contents until I saw a coupon on the back cover for a free mini-book. Since childhood, I had the habit of collecting free things from cereal boxes and other grocery boxes.

Each month when the magazine arrived I clipped another coupon, sent it in, and received another mini-book with titles such as *The New Birth*, *In Him* (teaching what it meant to be in Christ and how to be filled with the Spirit), *The Art of Intercession*, and more.

As I read those mini-books, redemptive realities became more real and clearer to me. I continued to read my Bible, finding verses that addressed my soul's issues. James 1:21 says, "Receive with meekness the engrafted word which is able to save your soul."

Romans 12:2 says "Be transformed by the renewing of your mind..."

I memorized Philippians 4:6-8 and companion verses such as 1 Peter 5:7 and Isaiah 26:3, which says "You will keep him in perfect peace whose mind is stayed on you."

Gradually fear was being replaced by faith and trust as I learned to act on God's Word, allowing God's Word to be my final authority rather than fearful lies.

For the insecurity issues, I memorized Psalm 139 which speaks of God and his careful involvement in our creation.

Daily I faced myself in the mirror and spoke aloud what God said about me, making confessions of the truth like "I'm fearfully and wonderfully made, God's works are marvelous and that my soul knows full well."

At first, I felt like a liar. The fact is I still "felt" insecure, but truth trumps fact when we choose to live by faith and not by sight. Soon a transformation began to happen. Knowledge of the truth of who I was in Christ was the key to my victory, and speaking these truths activated that key.

The Bible says "God's words are spirit and they are life... they are living and active." (John 6:63, Hebrews 4:12)

God's divine power is released into our lives by faith confession. By confessing with my mouth I was acknowledging the truths that caused these spiritual blessings to be activated into manifested realities.

My sisters tell me I began to blossom like a rose. I became more aware of the needs of others around me. I no longer focused only on myself and my inadequacies.

Helpful also during this time was an old book I found on Mom's bookshelf. It was another autobiography written by Norman Vincent Peale titled *The Power of Positive Living*.

The contents so resonated with the positive changes I was experiencing. I was amazed to discover that Mr. Peale, known as one of the world's most famous speakers, had overcome an inferiority complex too. He was once very shy and filled with self-doubt. He said he lived like a scared rabbit!

When he was a teenager his father took him for a walk in the woods. Together they sat on a log and talked. There his father directed him to Christ as the cure for what his father described as a "sensitive self-centeredness which lies at the root of inferiority-inadequacy feelings." He encouraged Norman to let Jesus take charge of his mind, emotions, and indeed his whole life.

"You could be freed of this misery," his father added. "If you let it continue, it can destroy your effectiveness." Norman Vincent Peale experienced deliverance through the positive power of submitting and committing his life to Jesus Christ.

I so identified with Mr. Peale's experience, I eagerly shared the book with my girlfriend. The following Sunday she handed it back to me with a grave look on her face. "Did you read it?" I asked. "No." She said, "My dad (who was a minister in our church) said I should not read it, and that positive thinking stuff is a false cult." I later heard my girlfriends were concerned that I was going "religious crazy," but despite their false perceptions, I continued in my quest to grow spiritually and socially.

* Horse and buggy Mennonite church my mother attended

* Lancaster County "black bumper" Mennonite church

CHAPTER 8

Sweet Sixteen

WITH THREE TEENAGE GIRLS AND ONE FAMILY CAR AT OUR HOUSE, DAD RECOGNIZED IT WAS TIME TO "BUY THE GIRLS A CAR."

He announced this one Saturday morning after breakfast. He then drove off to do the car shopping for us.

I was too young to remember when my dad sold our family's horse and buggy and bought a car. He transitioned the family to another Mennonite church, but it was still considered Old Order and very conservative. They allowed for cars; however, the cars had to be black, which the church elders considered a humble color. Whenever Dad bought a new black car, I can remember seeing him pull it under the shade of the tree in the front yard, then take a bucket of black paint and a brush and proceed to paint the bumpers, hubcaps, door handles, and any chrome that shown shiny. The church was nicknamed by other Mennonite churches "The Black Bumper Church."

Throughout the morning, Ruth, Eva Mae, and I tried to stay busy with the weekly cleaning, but we had trouble concentrating on our work. We felt nervous and anxious about Dad's choice of a model. "Oh, I do hope he doesn't buy us an old Pappy's car!" I moaned to Eva Mae.

Several hours later we met upstairs in our bedroom and discussed the benefit of having our own car. We would still have to share but we would work it out. Since Ruth and Eva Mae worked at the same sewing factory in Ephrata, they could drive together during the week. On the weekend we would take turns.

Just when I felt I could hardly stand the suspense, I looked out the window once more. That's when I noticed a small black car slowly cross over the bridge, then it slowed down to turn into our driveway. It was Dad and he was driving a nifty 1974 Ford Mustang, I felt giddy with relief!

"Dad's home!" I hollered. We raced down the stairs and burst into the kitchen just as Dad came through the kitchen screen door. "Where did you get the car?" Ruth calmly asked Dad.

"Got it at Philips Ford in Manheim for $2,000.00." He grumbled. Then added pleasantly "Well, go see how you like it."

We hurried out the door and down the walkway to our waiting beauty. Ruth and Eva Mae settled into the front seats and I climbed into the back. We "oohed" and "aahed" at the nice red interior. I noticed the mustang horse emblem on the steering wheel and suggested we call the Mustang "Billy." I also noticed dad had already cut the wires to the built-in radio. Our church did not allow for radios because of their possible negative influence. It was common practice to either remove the radio or detach the wires.

We drove Billy around the block and decided he would do just fine. Then the arguing began. Who was going to have the first turn to drive Billy this weekend? It was decided Ruth would drop me and Eva Mae off to meet our gang then, when Ruth's boyfriend Carl drove on their dates, Eva Mae could drive Billy.

I was fifteen and I would soon get my learner's permit. I was allowed to hang out with my girlfriends on Sunday afternoons but not in the evenings until I was sixteen. I looked forward to that privilege.

One Monday morning, on my way to feed the calves

in the heifer barn, I noticed something written in soap on Billy's back window. I got closer and blushed when I read "Ray Loves Elva."

My heart jumped inside my chest. Was this a silly prank my friends pulled on me or was there really a Ray who liked me? I was determined to solve this mystery. I quickly tried to erase the words, but just then, Ruth came down the walkway to go to work with her packed lunch box in her hand.

"You are too young for that stuff." She admonished and climbed into Billy and drove off to work.

All during chores, I puzzled over the message. Who was this Ray anyway? I didn't even know a guy by that name! That evening I called my friend Kendra and told her about the message. She told me her older sister said he belonged to another church and that his dad was a preacher. That was all she knew. This information just added to the mystery of the message!

Shortly after that, another friend devised a plan for Kendra and me to go with her to the local roller skating rink on a Sunday afternoon.

I felt slightly uncomfortable about the plan and so was Kendra. "Awe come on, there's nothing wrong with roller skating," Ellen said.

I knew there was no sin in roller skating, but deceiving our parents was wrong. Kendra had told her mom she was going to my house and I told my mom that I was going to Kendra's house. Then, when Ellen picked us up, we lay on the floor of the van so no one would see us. At the rink, we thoroughly enjoyed the skating, but the music and disco lights felt a bit too "worldly." Deep down, my conscience bothered me about the deception.

We skated until we had blisters on our feet. Near the end of the afternoon, I noticed two guys standing by the entrance waiting for us. Kendra skated alongside me and whispered, "It's him. That's Ray." I was suddenly very nervous as we skated to a stop and said "Hi" to his friend. I didn't have the courage to even look at Ray.

That was our first meeting. I later found out Ray was a year older than I was. He didn't realize I was so young, not yet sixteen. One Wednesday evening, after a spelling bee at the local fire hall, he asked me out. But I didn't feel I was ready to date so I said, "Not yet."

At age sixteen I was finally allowed to run around with the young people from our church youth group, but I quickly grew bored with the many volleyball games and what we called "crowd suppers" and "hops," where several hundred youths would gather from various districts. The parents provided us with a delicious supper. We would play volleyball and other games on the property, boys and girls would get acquainted, and occasionally a boy would ask to drive a girl home.

In the spring of my sixteenth year, Ray asked me out once more. This time it was at the Harrisburg relief sale, which was a benefit auction for disaster relief. Sometime after the evening's activities, one of the girls in my gang whispered in my ear, "Ray told me to ask you if he can take you home. And oh, by the way," she added with a grin, "he wears boots."

The girls in my gang had this thing about guys who wore cowboy boots! This time I accepted. We drove home in Kendra's boyfriend's pickup truck. We stopped for milkshakes at McDonald's. We didn't know what to say to our new boyfriends, so Kendra and I chit-chatted with each other all the way home. We even rehashed things we had talked about before just to fill the air with words and to avoid having to talk to our new boyfriends!

Later, at home, after Ray dropped me off, I strained to remember what he looked like. I only remembered his long eyelashes as I stole a sideways glance at him and oh yes, I remembered his cowboy boots.

I was still too young to date officially so Ray was not allowed to come to the house for our dates until I was sixteen and a half years old. So we occasionally met on Sunday afternoons throughout the summer and went hiking and such.

On weekend evenings I still hung out with the girls in my gang, attending birthday parties and sleepovers.

I started to grow bored with the gossip about boys and other drama.

One unforgettable sleepover I drew a line in the sand with the nonsense. The evening began with a pizza party at Ellen's house. The gang of giggling girls arrived with a plan: "Let's sneak off to the movies." one friend suggested. Immediately I felt uncomfortable. Not only did my parents not allow us to go to movies, but I had heard that the movie they planned to see had inappropriate content.

All during pizza I pondered what to do.

"I'm not going to go along," I finally told Ellen.

There, I said it. I felt instantly relieved until she laid into me and complained, "What am I supposed to do? I don't want to stay here with you and I can't let you here alone!" she finished exasperated.

"It's okay," I urged, "I don't mind staying here, really. You go on."

After the girls left, I felt alone... very alone. The big house was dark and empty so I went out to sit in my car and waited for the gang of girls to return. I watched a shiny sports car slowly drive by, then back again. I began to feel uneasy. The car passed again and turned around, this time it pulled alongside my car and rolled down the window, revealing it was the guys from our gang and my boyfriend! He asked in a concerned tone if I was all alone, wondering "Where is everyone else?"

"They went to the movies," I explained.

The guys offered to stay with me until the rest of the girls returned. But I assured them I was okay by myself. So away they drove into the night.

Before long a gang of sober girls returned from the movies. One friend whispered to me, "Be lucky you didn't go. It was a gross movie." Now I was the one who was smiling and truly lighthearted. My heart was free of a guilty conscience and I felt good inside and out.

We had barely settled into our sleeping bags on the parlor floor when suddenly the door flung open and a stinking dead possum came flying through the air, landing with a thud on a sleeping bag. We screamed and scampered out of the way, stumbling over each other in a run for the windows. We heard tires squeal, an engine revved, and we caught a glimpse in the moonlight of a black Mustang disappearing into the night. This meant war! We scooped up the dead possum put him in a garbage bag and piled into Ellen's van and hurried off into the night. The guys were sleeping over at my boyfriend's house, so we parked nearby and waited and waited for them to park their cars and for the lights to go off in the house. Stealthily we snuck up the driveway and placed the possum on a freshly polished black sports car. The dog barked and we hightailed it for the van.

As I remember the unfolding of events that night, several more times the possum took a trip back and forth in the van until we decided we'd better get some sleep since we had to attend church the next morning.

It was a very sleepy but content group of teenagers that slipped into church that Sunday morning; we would never forget those fun memories from our "running around" days as long as we lived.

* My "gang" of girl friends

CHAPTER 9

A Life-altering Experience

THE PHONE RANG.

It was my cousin Mary inviting me to go with her and the family she did babysitting for to Elverson Mennonite Church to hear an evangelist preach.

"I don't think I can go, I have to milk the cows this weekend because Mom and Dad are away visiting Uncle

Irvin's in New York," I explained.

"Can't you milk a bit earlier and still make it to the meeting?" she suggested.

I hurried with the evening chores. All went well milking Dad's herd of 50 cows. I scrubbed myself to get rid of the barn smell, got into my Sunday cape dress, hurriedly pinned on my prayer covering, then dashed out the door and drove off to the meeting. As I drove I had a sense that this would be a special evening.

We arrived in the middle of worship. The music and singing were something quite like I never experienced before. At our church, musical instruments were not allowed. The singing was somber and slow with a sorrowful feeling.

This evangelist talked about God as if he could be your friend and you could hear his voice in your heart. This was somewhat of a new concept to me. I'd been reading about this in the mini-books I'd collected from the Word of Faith ministry. In that meeting, I saw demonstrations of the manifestations of the gifts of the Spirit I had been reading about in the Bible in the book of Acts. This intrigued me. I was taught that healing and miracles and the gifts of the Spirit were "done away with," something only meant for the early church but not the church today.

I could not accept that line of thinking, so my heart was open. Still, it was a bit frightening. I looked over at

Cousin Mary.

"You look scared," she said to me in Dutch.

All around us strange things were happening spontaneously, but in a peaceful and orderly manner. Nearby, a lady was praying for someone else and the person was healed on the spot.

"How is that possible?" I puzzled. The lady was wearing pants! "How could the power of God work through her when she was wearing jeans?" Even if I didn't understand it, my heart was hungry and eager to learn.

For the remainder of the weekend, I hurried through chores and raced off to all the meetings with Cousin Mary. On the final night of the meeting, the speaker gave an invitation for people to receive Christ. I had already done that I realized, but somehow I knew there was something I needed. I was missing something.

During the second invitation, my heart began to pound within in my chest; I knew I needed to respond, but I so very much did not want to go up front. The evangelist continued to invite people to come forward and receive.

My knuckles turned white as I held tightly to the back of the pew in front of me. I felt compelled to go up. Slowly I moved out of the pew. By the time I reached the front, the tears flowed freely as I surrendered. The ladies gathered around me to lay hands on me and pray for me. I never had anyone pray for me before; it was a beautiful experience. When they determined that I was already born again they prayed that I would be baptized in the Holy Spirit. When I lifted my head and my heart to God to receive, I saw a bright light from above descend upon me and fill my whole being. It must have affected my countenance because the pastor sitting in the front row called out, "She's got it, She's got it!" Everyone around me rejoiced!

It is difficult to explain spiritual experiences in natural terms, but what I experienced that night so changed my life. My family immediately noticed the difference. Several days later I sat in my parlor reading my Bible, enjoying the presence of God when my sister Eva Mae entered and sat on the sofa next to me.

"Okay, what's up," she blurted out. "Something's happened to you. You are different and whatever it is I want it too."

She began to weep and cry; instinctively I reached out to lay my hands on her knee and prayed for her to receive the Holy Spirit. Instantly her hands shot upwards to heaven and she began to freely praise the Lord in a heavenly language. I was rather startled and amazed at the same time. This must be the language of the Spirit I read about in the Bible! I had also received that ability and how refreshing it was to pray in the Spirit instead of what used to feel like empty-headed praying from my natural mind. I experienced the reality of Jude 1:20 exhorts us to "Build yourselves on your most holy faith, praying in the Holy Ghost." When I prayed in the Spirit I literally felt as though my "spiritual batteries" were being "charged up"!

On our next date, my boyfriend said the same thing that my sister said.

"Something happened to you; you're different."

I told him the whole story of what happened at the meetings and my experience with my sister and the unspeakable joy and spiritual fulfillment I was experiencing. Ray was very interested and asked for more explanation. Together we read the New Testament and ministry materials that explained this wonderful phenomenon referred to as "the second work of grace" or "the baptism in the Holy Spirit." He too received the baptism in the Holy Spirit during his own quiet time with the Lord. While I understood the work of the Holy Spirit in the new birth experience, I knew there was a difference between having the Spirit and being "filled" with the Spirit.

I noticed an increased awareness of a "calling"; a desire to share the good news of the Gospel. As I prayed about that awareness and explored it, I continued to share what I had discovered with those around me. I met with another cousin for lunch at her house; before the afternoon was over she asked me to pray with her. She too received the filling of the Spirit.

I was on a roll! Being instrumental in a work of God in another person's life was more fulfilling than anything I had ever experienced! I went from sisters to sister-in-laws and prayed for opportunities to share with my friends from church.

It was the season for water baptism at our church. Every spring and fall the youth attended instructional classes to prepare for baptism and learn the Mennonite church doctrine. We called it "joining the church" it was to be a somber occasion. We had to wear black dresses and black stockings.

My friends whined and complained about having to attend classes and wear black stockings. Nor did their hearts seem to understand the significance of water baptism.

I looked forward to the Sunday morning of our baptism, our class sat in the front pew. The minister finished his sermon and we knelt before him. The bishop's wife untied our head coverings, then the bishop proceeded to sprinkle water over our heads. Tears mingled with the water as it ran down my cheeks. I pictured Christ's death on the cross for my sin. My heart was full of wonder and gratitude. When the Bishop reached for my hand and said, "Rise to a new life, a new beginning," I stood up with a big smile on my face. To me, it was a special spiritual experience, but outside the church house, my friends mocked and fussed about the length of the service and their hot black dresses. It hurt me deeply to see how nonchalant they were about such a significant service.

I began to pray for my friends and look for opportunities to share with them. Previously, since our church did not have Sunday school or Bible studies, Kendra and I started a Bible study with a few friends on a Sunday afternoon. It grew quickly from four in attendance to eleven, then 22 girls. That's when we sought out the help of an older single woman from the church. Mysteriously, the following Sunday, attendance quickly declined as girls, one by one, told us they were no longer allowed to attend. Their parents were concerned their daughters would be led astray at Bible study. So Kendra and I continued on our own.

One Sunday morning, as the congregation sang the closing hymn, I whispered to Kendra behind the hymnbook, "I have something really exciting to tell you, can we talk this afternoon?"

"Oh, I'd love to," she whispered back, "But I can't. I have to go to a family reunion today, but let's talk next Sunday afternoon."

We were not allowed to talk on the phone during the week, only briefly to make weekend plans. We had a party line and often other families needed the line too. Plus, we didn't like for others to listen in on our conversations, so we would have to wait to talk until next Sunday. I didn't think I could wait that long, so I just told her bits and pieces of my experience. Her eyes lit up "Oh, I want that too." she whispered.

"I'll explain it all next Sunday and show you the Scriptures I found," I assured her.

We parted after church with great anticipation of what God would accomplish in our friendship next Sunday.

Alas, when the next Sunday arrived, her demeanor had changed. She was no longer interested.

"I talked to my Mom about it," she explained. "Mom said that people who experience this go off the left wing and usually end up leaving the church." She went on to tell me about the evangelist Jim Bakker scandal she had just read about in the newspaper.

"Be careful about those worldly evangelists." She warned.

I felt confused. I didn't know who Jim Bakker was, but I held dear what I had experienced and determined not to let go of it.

Still, I was puzzled. I respected my friend and her mother, but how could this be wrong? I had no intention or desire to leave the church; I only had a desire to see spiritual revival happen in my church.

Something had shifted in our relationship. My girlfriend was no longer interested in discussing spiritual matters on the same level as I wanted to. I found myself spending more time with my cousins and less time with my church friends. When we double-dated with other couples in our gang, we couldn't enjoy the carnal country and rock music cassette tapes they played in their car as we drove.

We no longer enjoyed that kind of music. When Ray and I drove on our double dates, we played our new inspirational Gospel music tapes. A few minutes into the first song I heard giggles from the two couples in the back seat. One of the guys leaned forward and mockingly asked, "Did you guys get religious!?" The back seat erupted into laughter. We blushed and experienced what it felt like to be mocked for our faith.

Inside I felt grieved that things had changed in our relationships. As for Ray and I, my dad did not want me to date Ray and urged me to break up with him since he was from a more liberal Mennonite church. In my background, it was very important for families to worship in the same church. My family pressured me to make a decision.

"It's better to work out your differences before you get too serious about each other," They warned.

I wasn't sure what to do so we broke up for a bit, but the breakup only lasted a month; we were miserable apart. We knew we were meant for each other. Back together again, we still were uncertain as to whose church to attend. While we were apart, I studied a book titled *How Can You Know the Will of God?* While I didn't find the instant direction I was looking for, I discovered how to remain in peace until the answer was revealed. We decided to let the decision rest and not to worry about it. Perhaps things would be clearer for us down the road.

On our dates, I noticed Ray was not feeling well. He tried to be pleasant and shrugged off the frequent abdominal pains he was experiencing. He underwent a series of tests that did not reveal anything serious, only a small hernia which they scheduled to have removed.

Before the scheduled surgery, Ray fell violently ill. His parents rushed him to the ER. This time the test revealed a tumor in his intestines. An emergency surgery was scheduled to remove the tumor.

That night I tossed and turned and battled thoughts in my head. I tried to focus on my favorite verses. Once again the truth and power of Isaiah 26:3 came to mind; "You will keep him in perfect peace whose mind is stayed on you, because he trusts in you." Phil 4:6-8 was also a great comfort, which advises us to "Be anxious for nothing... the peace of God will guard your heart and mind.... Think on things above..."

I decided to pray and trust God for Ray's health.

To keep my mind from wandering all over the place, I prayed for others in need until I drifted off to sleep.

The next time I went to see Ray in the hospital he was not in the room. While I waited for his return I noticed a written note on his nightstand with lines, arrows, and illustrations next to the word CANCER. I tensed at the sight of the word and wondered what it could mean. When Ray was wheeled back to his room, he explained the note to me. The cancer was called Liposarcoma. The Doctor was confident the cancer was removed along with the tumor and six inches of intestines surrounding the tumor. Since the cancer was localized, he did not need further treatment. The next hurdle was to see if Ray's bowels would work again or if he would have to wear a bag for the rest of his life. We were greatly relieved when within several days his bowels began to work again.

When he returned from the hospital a week later he was very thin and weak, he weighed only 110 pounds. Gradually his weight and health returned. We were very grateful that Ray's life was spared.

CHAPTER 10

Teenager on a Mission

AGAIN THE PHONE RANG.

This time it was my cousin Lydia. She told me all about a mission trip and invited me to go along for the summer to the Indian reservations in northern Ontario to teach vacation Bible school. This sounded like a much more meaningful summer than running around with my girlfriends.

I just wasn't sure Dad would allow me to go; he depended on my help with the milking and the hay baling in the summertime.

I waited a few days and looked for the perfect time to ask Dad. He was usually in a better mood while milking his fine herd of Holsteins.

So, during the evening milking, I finally gathered up enough courage and asked if I could go.

He didn't answer but kept on chewing on the wad of tobacco in his cheek. My dad used to smoke cigars, but since his oldest brother died from lung cancer he was trying hard to stop smoking. Instead, he chewed tobacco.

"Please God," I prayed under my breath. Dad grunted and I stepped back as he spit another long stream of tobacco juice into the gutter.

"Well...I guess you could go. Aaron Ray is getting old enough to help out. How much does it cost?" he asked.

"Nothing," I quickly reassured him. I had already planned to pay for the trip myself.

I was stunned. I had Dad's permission to go on a mission trip! I would get to be a real missionary! I didn't agree with the preacher on Sunday when he piously stated, "We are missionaries with our plain humble black colored cars. We are a separate, peculiar people, and the world can see we belong to God." I cringed as he lengthily expounded on the virtues of the plain and simple life.

We had to provide the ministry with a letter of approval from parents or a pastor, in addition to another reference. I asked Kendra if she could send a letter of recommendation to the ministry. My cousin Mary told me later she peeked at the letter before sending it and it was full of warnings of our errant ways and our involvement in a "false cult." Even so, we were accepted! Little did my cousins realize, this decision would later cost them excommunication from their horse and buggy Old Order Mennonite church!

I prepared, with great anticipation, for the summer away from home. I had never traveled this far before. When feelings of apprehension came I read Joshua 1:9 ..."Be strong and courageous, do not be afraid, nor be dismayed, for the Lord your God is with you wherever you go." I also kept myself built up by praying in the Spirit.

I said goodbye to Ray and promised to write. Mom followed me to the door and said "God's blessings." and gave me a holy kiss on the cheek. Our family did not hug or kiss each other. This was the first display of affection I can remember.

Cousin Lydia, Mary, and I met with the other teammates from Pennsylvania, all of whom were strangers to us, but we quickly got acquainted and piled in a large maxi van. As we approached the border of Canada I got out my Bible and read those comforting verses again. At long last, we arrived in Dryden, Ontario at Beaver Lake Ministries, the headquarters for Northern Youth Programs. Since long-distance calls were expensive, we were only allowed to make one very brief phone call home to let our families know we had arrived safely.

When I heard Mom's voice on the other end I felt a twinge of homesickness.

"How's the weather in Canada?" She asked.

"Nice, a bit chilly," I told her and soon hung up the receiver.

For the first week, we stayed at headquarters for a time of training. We learned the basics of the Native culture and how to teach Bible school to children. We even learned how to make Indian bread on an open fire. At the end of the week, we received our assignments. We were told to pack light and to prepare a box of food. We were to be flown out to the reservations in a small float plane, two by two.

I was both nervous and excited. I'd never flown in a plane before, but I was determined not to be in fear about it. I took a deep breath and climbed into the backseat with my teammate Mandy, who was a stranger to me, but not for long.

The small single-engine plane skimmed across the lake and lifted off, up over the treetops. After a 30-minute flight, we landed on a lake and taxied up to the beach of the Lac Sual Indian reservation. Children with bright eager faces stared as we climbed down from the plane. I clutched my box as the pilot said,

"Goodbye, see you in a few weeks."

I stood on the beach and watched the plane fly off and

disappear in the sky, a feeling came over me I will never forget. "Now whats" and "what ifs" tried to control my mind. Instead, I focused on the task before us and Jesus' words: "I will never leave you or forsake you.... lo I'm with you always..."

The chief introduced himself to us and walked us to the hut where we would stay. It was a tiny house with thin walls, a tiny kitchen, and a sitting room, and off to the side were two bunk beds.

The hut was very dirty, so first we cleaned and made up our beds. All the while, children milled around our doorstep. We decided to get acquainted with the children by going on a walk with them and invited them to VBS, which we told them would be held on the beach down by the lake. The children grabbed our hands and said in their thick native accents, "Come, we show you something."

We wound around a wooded path and followed it to a small cliff overlooking the lake. To me, the beautiful vista looked peaceful in the evening light of the setting sun. The children played among the rocks, but when the sun set suddenly the children looked frightened.

"Hurry, we must go back before dark," an older boy urged. Then he pointed out across the lake to a small island beyond.

"That's devil's island," he explained. "After dark, the demons come out in fire and smoke," he finished with ever-widening eyes.

We hurried back through the woods to our summer home and said goodnight to the children.

Once inside, Mandy and I sat on the sofa and began our plans for our summer of teaching. "What are we going to do? You got any materials with you?"

I'd never been to Sunday school or vacation Bible school in all my life! I looked to my teammate for support since she grew up in a church that had Sunday schools.

Mandy had been on a mission trip before so she told me of a missionary family that lived across the lake.

"Perhaps we could go visit them tomorrow and see if they had any supplies for us to use." She suggested.

Weary from our day's travels, we decided to turn in early. We visited the tiny rustic outhouse behind the hut.

Back inside, Mandy suggested, "Let's pray before we go to bed."

"Good idea," I quickly agreed.

We prayed for the children and our safety and "plead the blood of Jesus" around our little hut.

After the prayers, Mandy went to the kitchen and came back with a big butcher knife. In a puzzled tone I asked, "What do you plan to do with that thing?"

Without a word, she walked over to the only door and slid the blade of the knife through the door frame to serve as a lock.

"Well, that can't hurt." I thought to myself.

In peaceful confidence, I snuggled under the covers. Canadian nights were chillier than summer nights in PA. Soon I drifted off to sleep.

Suddenly, I was awakened by a shaking motion and banging sound, but I couldn't tell where the noise was coming from. It seemed to come from every direction at once.

"You okay?" I called out to Mandy in a weak voice.

"Pray," she whispered back.

I felt a choking sensation as fear gripped my mind. Under the blanket, I whispered my verses over and over to comfort myself.

"The Lord is my shepherd... yea though I walk through the valley and the shadow...." then closed my eyes.

Before long, all was quiet again. I stayed under the covers and somehow fell back to sleep.

The next morning Mandy and I investigated the door. The knife was still there. Nothing was out of place outside, and all was as it should be. We realized it was "spiritual warfare" as Mandy called it.

"Yes, well," I declared, "According to 1 John 4:4, 'Greater is He that is in us than he that is in the world!'"

That day we got into a boat and rowed out across the lake to the missionary's home. The Millers warmly greeted us and expressed joy at seeing fellow Americans. They prepared a nice lunch for us, after which we sat and chatted, getting acquainted. Finally, we got around to explaining the reason for our visit.

"So, we were wondering if you had any supplies here we could borrow to help us teach VBS in Lac Sual?" Mandy led.

Mrs. Miller grinned knowingly and replied, "Well, how about you tell us what you need and we'll tell you how to do without it!" She finished with a laugh.

Then, seriously this time, she offered some ideas and sent pencils and paper with us, but no curriculum or visual aids or anything else that would make our task easier. I realized in a new way why it's so important to support mission work with our finances and resources.

I would have to pray and prepare. I looked to God for help. For resources, I looked at nature around me. I had sticks and stones and, thankfully, my guitar. We would just have to make do.

When I was 12 years old, I snuck into my brother's bedroom while he was at work and strummed on his guitar. In time I taught myself a few basic chords from the instructional book I found in the case. When my brother heard how well I could play, he let me have the instrument. I loved music and wanted the guitar with me for my personal enjoyment on my trip away from home, but suddenly I realized it could serve as a ministry tool.

I decided to teach about creation. I prepared children's songs and Bible verses for the children to memorize. I practiced a dramatic Bible story reading, games, and a snack. This would have to do for our VBS program!

A large group of excited children of various ages met us on the beach by the lake. Mandy and I divided them into two groups. I took mine to a little grove of trees nearby and sat them down in the grass. I introduced myself and our plan for the week, then began my Bible lesson. I waved my arms out across the lake pointing to creation and asked, "Who made all this?"

As I expounded on the wonders of God and his creation, their eyes glazed over in incomprehension. Boredom overcame them and they wiggled and squirmed as I taught them theological concepts too complex for their understanding. Realizing this wasn't working, my lesson came to a quick end and I hurriedly transitioned to a time of singing. Suddenly I had their full attention. The children loved my guitar. They jumped and clapped and willingly learned new songs.

Whew, we did it! Back at our hut, we collapsed in our chairs. Teaching children was exhausting. We prepared the next day's lesson and began to work on a closing program for later in the week. We decided to invite parents and have hot dogs and a bonfire on the beach.

We filled the remainder of our time visiting with the women on the reservation. At one point our next-door neighbor invited us to tea. She served us tea and cakes and shared her concerns for the Native young people. She expressed that they felt as though they didn't have much to live for. Many were lonely and depressed; they sniffed glue to get high to escape their miserable reality. This made me very sad and urged me to pray more on their behalf.

* My team picture, taken prior to our departure for home

CHAPTER 11

Row for your Life!

ANOTHER EVENING A SMALL NATIVE FAMILY INVITED US TO DINNER.

We had an enjoyable time as they cooked us a fine meal and proudly showed us around their small, but tidy, pleasant home. To us, they seemed like a happy, healthy family.

Several days later the neighbor knocked on our door.

"Come, hurry," she spoke in an urgent tone. "Come to the beach, the women and children are being evacuated. The local drunk is on a rampage, it looks bad."

We raced after her down to the lake. Mandy and I jumped into our boat and rowed as fast as we could across the lake. After we landed we pulled the boat up on the beach and ran for cover in a nearby empty hut. We locked the door and pulled the shades, then waited in silence.

Mandy suggested we go over the ministry prayer list to pass the time. We took turns praying for the names on the list. This not only passed the time but provided a good outlet for fearful thoughts that tried to dominate our minds. Before long we heard distant shouts and gunfire. The noise was getting closer and closer.

Mandy looked at me worriedly and said, "Come, let's hide under the bed."

She pulled me down onto the dusty dirty floor as the shouting, cursing, and gunfire drew closer. I pulled myself up to peek out the window. It was a pitiful scene of a life out of control. I'd never seen the effects of alcohol before. I felt compassion for the wretched soul... he cursed loudly while shooting in the windows and flower pots on the doorsteps of the house next door, calling his wife's name and threatening to shoot everyone in sight.

"Get down! He'll see you and come after us," Mandy urged loudly.

We heard a motorboat pull up to the dock and the shouts of authority. This time Mandy peeked.

"It's the police," she said in a relieved tone. We watched as they tackled and handcuffed the drunken man, then took him away in the motor boat.

Outside, the Native women and children slowly came out of hiding, including the drunk's wife and two young whimpering girls holding tightly to their mother's skirt.

"He's not usually like this, really he's not!" she sobbed. To my dismay, I realized it was the beautiful young family we had dinner with only several nights earlier. We held her hand and tried to console her.

"They will get your husband some help and we will pray for him," we said.

Somberly, we rowed back with the other women and children and then walked her to her home. The tidy little house was in shambles with broken dishes strewn across the floor. The furniture was shattered. This scene was all too familiar for the women and children on the reservation.

Our time in Lac Sual was coming to an end. We would soon be sent to another reservation for another two weeks of teaching. I tried to put as much Bible information into the children as possible in such a short time and prayed they would receive the love of God. On the day after the closing program, I was in the hut packing our belongings when I heard a faint little knock on our door.

"Well hello," I said to the little boy standing outside the door. "What can I do for you?"

With his hands behind his back he shyly asked, "Would you sing church songs for me like we sang in Bible school?"

"Why certainly!" I replied. "I'll get my guitar and be right out."

We sat down on the steps, the boy sitting close by me. Oh, what to sing? I searched my memory and, strumming the chords, began to sing:

"I have decided to follow Jesus..." After the last chorus, I turned to him and asked, "Have you done that? I mean, have you invited Jesus into your heart and decided to follow him?"

A smile crossed his tanned face as he replied, "Oh yes. I did, just last week."

My heart glowed at the thought of this being one of the fruits of our labor. A soul was saved; a heart changed! It so thrilled my heart that I prayed a prayer of promise to God.

"Lord, I don't want to live life unto myself. I always want to serve you in one way or another."

The next morning we said goodbye to the children on the beach. We were flown in the small float plane back to headquarters to restock. We were given a day off before going on to the next reservation.

My cousins and I decided to row a canoe out to a giant rock beneath the trees to sunbathe and write letters to the folks back home. We packed food, sleeping bags, and stationary, and rowed out to the rocky island. We spread out the sleeping bags and sat crossed legged and began to write. First I wrote to my boyfriend. I felt a twinge of homesickness again as I realized how much I missed him. I wrote all about our time on the reservation.

I was so engrossed in the silent conversation that I had not noticed the sun slip behind the clouds. Across the lake, it looked like a giant storm cloud was coming our way. We realized we had better head back. Quickly we gathered up our things, climbed into the canoe, and began to row. Soon we could hear the sounds of rain in the distance, and then we felt it on our backs. Faster and harder we rowed. Suddenly it seemed as though we were engulfed in layers of driving rain, and we lost sight of the shore. Were we going in the right direction?

"Keep going straight!" Lydia shouted from the back I was steering in the front of the canoe and doing my best to keep a straight course. Fears of "what ifs" mocked me in my mind as I rowed.

I reminded myself, "The Lord is my helper, my strength, and my song, he has become my salvation..." Bump!

We all lurched forward. We were so blinded by the rain that we couldn't see it coming... we had rowed right into the dock at the shores of Beaver Lake!

The guys were already there preparing canoes to come to our rescue. They helped us out of our canoe and carried our heavy, water-logged sleeping bags. The love letter I had written to Ray was soaked through and through. It was no good, I had to trash it.

We were relieved and grateful for our caring teammates and our God who promises in Psalm 46:1 to be a, "very present help in times of trouble."

* *Writing letters back home*

CHAPTER 12

Savant Lake

I WAS SENT OUT AGAIN FOR TWO MORE WEEKS,

this time with Cousin Mary to another reservation. We were transported by vehicle instead of by plane. Mary's Old Order horse-and-buggy Mennonite church did not permit their members to fly airplanes, so the directors of the ministry sent us to Savant Lake.

There we settled into another small hut which the locals informed us was haunted. We shrugged off the comment and focused on our mission. Our house was situated near a beautiful lake which was our water source. We drank the lake water, bathed in the lake, wash our clothes in the lake, and oh yes, we swam in the lake too! This natural setting inspired Mary to write a beautiful poem titled "Canada."

It's the land of the lakes where the fish leap high,
Where the snow gets deep and the pine trees sigh.
Where the natives still trap and live off the land.
Still the Indian chief does what's best for his band.
The sky is so clear and the loons give their call,
While the wolves roam the forest in the cool splendid fall.
It's the place to go when you're tired of the rush,
And somehow draw closer to the God you trust.
The One who still reigns on His throne up above,
Yet dwells in our hearts too, as we walk in His love.

As soon as Mary and I settled in, we endeavored to get acquainted with the youth in the area. We quickly befriended a lonely young single mother. For me, this was a new experience. I never met a single-parent family before. I quickly noticed the lack of balance in the family unit and realized the beauty of God's design for the family to consist of father, mother, and children.

While Tina regretted her past sins, at first she wasn't

willing to change her lifestyle and wanted to continue to hang out and hook up with other men, which caused one complicated mess after another.

"Sin brings sorrow into our lives," we explained. "Life is so much better when we do it God's way."

We continued to meet with her on a regularly for fellowship and Bible studies. Eventually, Tina and her young son's difficult situation was redeemed when she learned to turn to God as her source for her needs life.

We tried to organize volleyball games with the youth but found it very frustrating to work with their ideas of time in the Indian culture. We would schedule something and they would show up hours later; it was virtually impossible to stay on schedule.

On other days we did door-to-door visitation, carrying with us a backpack filled with books about family life and relationships, Bibles, cassette tapes, and Gospel tracks from the ministry. We knocked on the door of a tiny home. A smiling lady greeted us and graciously invited us inside. She insisted we stay to visit and seated us at her kitchen table. She bustled around her tiny kitchen, chatting all the while as she served us coffee... dark, black, bitter coffee. I never had coffee before so I took a tiny sip and decided I didn't like it very much, but I couldn't turn down her offer. I felt it best, while on the mission field, to eat and drink what was set before me.

Thankfully she served tiny tea cakes with the coffee. I tried not to squint my eyes as I sipped the bitter liquid and helped it down with plenty of cakes. On and on she talked. She was so happy for visitors and wanted us to stay longer. She eagerly poured us more coffee. I couldn't say "no thanks" and spoil her fun! So I drank more coffee. Not being used to so much caffeine, I stayed awake long into the night long after we parted ways and stared at the ceiling, listening to the wind in the swaying trees outside.

When we returned to headquarters, we happily discovered Cousin Lydia had fallen in love! It all happened when Jim Miller, another team member, asked her for a haircut. In the process, they got acquainted and discovered they liked each other. In a week of recap, we reunited with all the other teams and shared stories of our experiences on the reservations.

Our summer of service was coming to an end. My heart ached to see Ray again, and I longed to see the home farm. While I was excited to return home, I felt so privileged to have experienced this taste of the missionary's life. It changed my perception of the world outside of the church culture. Little did I realize what was happening in the church back home and that something both wonderful and chaotic awaited me there.

* Trying our hand at canoeing on Savant Lake

* Mandy and me with our vacation Bible school class

CHAPTER 13

What are you Thinking?

IT FELT SO GOOD TO BE HOME AGAIN.

"Absence makes the heart grow fonder," Ray said. I do believe he was right. We grew closer in our relationship during our absence. By now we had been dating just a little over three years. Marriage was not yet in sight, but I knew it was getting closer.

On a Saturday shortly after my return from Canada, Ray took me on a date to see a local air show. I was aware of Ray's interest in airplanes as he had expressed from time to time his desire to learn to fly. The concept was so foreign to me that I dismissed it from my mind. Ray however actively began looking into the possibility.

He told me that one Sunday after church he approached the bishop and asked him what he thought about an aviation career.

"Our people don't do that," he said, he didn't recommend that kind of a career.

Ray consulted his parents as well. They felt since it was so expensive to train to fly it would be best if Ray would save his money for a future home. Ray was in his element at the airport. We looked at all the planes and watched the mighty display of the blue angels in flight. It was a lovely day together, but when we returned home we noticed a big black car sitting in the driveway of my parents' home and two dark-clothed men stood in the yard talking to my dad. When I saw who it was, a sinking feeling appeared in the pit of my stomach. Sure enough, my dad met me as I approached the yard.

"The Deacon and the Bishop are here to talk to you," He said with a tense look on his face.

Dad went back to the barn to tend to the cows and Ray

went to wait for me inside. I stood in the yard and faced the two men alone. The Bishop cleared his throat and explained the purpose of their visit.

"We hear," he said, "That you've been going to Bible studies, and listening to preachers that wear neckties and their wives wear lipstick and earrings. Do you know these preachers only preach things people want to hear and don't preach all the truth? You need to promise to stop listening to them and to stop reading their materials."

I was astonished and wasn't sure how to respond. Just then I saw our plain neighbor girl bike past our place, she was from a church even more conservative than ours. I suddenly realized the essence of their request and answered, "What you are asking, then, is much the same as her Bishop asking her not to listen to you. The ministers I listen to are Christians and preachers of the Gospel, even though you don't see some things in the same way. Still, they profess Christ, and Jesus is in them as he is in you, therefore we can't push each other out. If we do so we are pushing part of Jesus out."

The Deacon stood by, nervously turning his hat over and over in his hands. Finally he said, "If you keep going on the path that you're going, you can't be a member of our church."

"That's right," the Bishop continued, "if we do not hear of your decision by next Sunday you will be put off the church."

This was a grave prospect. Plain churches were considered to be their own individual culture, and stepping from one to the other was considered to be a blatant rejection of your former community.

He then placed his broad-brimmed black hat on his head and turned to leave. The Deacon followed him to their car.

I turned to walk to the house trying to process the ultimatum I was just given, but by the time I reached the front door, I had committed it to God and decided to trust him for the answer. By now I had learned when I didn't know what to do or how to pray, I prayed in the Spirit, and immediately peace and calm came over me.

When Ray and I said our goodbyes later that evening he looked a bit preoccupied, so I asked him, "What are you thinking?"

"Oh it's nothing," He replied.

"It is too," I insisted. "What are you thinking?"

"Alright then," he grinned, "I was wondering if you would marry me."

Wow! Even though I was a bit surprised by the question, and maybe not quite ready for engagement, I knew the answer right away and said, "Sure I would!" We decided to take the year to prepare and then get married that next October.

I had a lot to think about that week. I thought about the

call to the Bishop. What would life be like for me if I would do as he wished? I desired the approval of the church elders, and especially that of my father. "God, what do you want me to do?" was the prayer of my heart.

The same weekend of the deadline for the decision, Cousin Lydia and her boyfriend Jim, Ray, and I already had plans to assist in an evangelical Mennonite church planting effort in New York City. We assisted the pastor with extending invitations to make people aware of the new church. The noise of the city was almost overwhelming to me as people scurried about in all directions.

We approached a homeless man sitting on a park bench and asked if we could pray for him. He looked at us curiously and asked if we were Hutterites.

"No, we are Christians and we are here to pray for you," I said, handing him a Gospel tract and an invitation to the church.

"I'll bet you are Quakers, or Amish, or something like that," he insisted. "Tell me about the Amish..." He went on and on with curious surface questions about why they don't have electricity and drive horse and buggy and why we wore those things on our heads. Suddenly, I realized he was being distracted by our plain looks and head coverings. Did he think we were trying to convert him into our way of life and therefore, not interested in our message?

I felt for the first time a desire to be free from the looks that distinguished us as a part of Mennonite doctrine, which I was beginning to feel, at least in part, was man's religion and not something God required of us. It was a frustrating effort to try to point him to the message of the cross.

Since I wasn't at our home church that morning, I asked Mom when I returned home, "Well, what did they say?"

"They did it. They put you off the church," She replied with little emotion. From the beginning, Mom seemed to have an understanding concerning the spiritual revival her children were experiencing since she too had a similar experience. She didn't like man-made denominational lines, but often quoted a line from an old song... "You go to your church and I'll go to mine, and we'll walk together side by side."

I went to my bedroom, sat on the bed, and sighed. I felt an unusual lightness both inside and out. I considered where I might worship next Sunday.

When Dad realized I was not coming back to the Mennonite church and that six of his nine children were also being excommunicated for the same reason I was, he became uncontrollably upset. He began to try to control and manipulate us with threats of removing us from his will and inheritance.

I began to see a side of my dad that made me

very uncomfortable.

The Bishop told him, "You're the priest of your home, and therefore you must control your household." The church members blamed my father's leadership.

Dad worried about the future of the farm and what could happen to his children and grandchildren if they did not stay in the Mennonite faith. He predicted that there would be divorces in the family, even perhaps drugs and alcohol abuse and all manner of evil outside the safe confines of his denomination.

He stormed the house, confiscating any books or magazines that did not come from his church. He searched my parlor and bedroom; he took my praise and worship cassettes and smashed them to bits with a sledgehammer and threw them on the manure spreader. He became consumed in his efforts to change the circumstances that were out of his control.

He carefully watched the mailbox and did not allow us to get the mail. Nor did he allow Mom to go away with us.

I felt so bad for Dad. For the sake of peace, I always tried to please him as best I could. I would often give up my rights and will to do so. However, in this matter I had a higher authority to answer to; I remained resolute in my decision. My married sibling came to talk to Dad to try and help him understand the workings of God in our lives. This only upset

Dad even more.

Every time church members talked to him, he became unhinged and even unsafe. I kept my distance as best I could. The chaos continued for a few months until eventually, it climaxed into a need for help when Dad made suicide threats if we didn't do as he wished.

I was very concerned. In tears, I went to the telephone and called my oldest brother Paul and told him what Dad had said.

That evening, after milking and while Dad was still in the barn, a police car drove into the driveway. The sight made me feel sick but inside I knew we needed help. My little brother, now twelve years old, was outback feeding his rabbits.

He did not see the police car coming. I did not want him to have this sight in his memory, so I hurried out the back door to find him and told him to quickly come inside with me. I took him through my parlor, then to the back porch where he couldn't see the car. Up to this point, Aaron Ray was somewhat unaware of our family's problems. Previously, Dad tried to control himself around his youngest child.

I put my arm around him and explained as best I could that Dad needed help. "He's being taken to the hospital," I explained.

Aaron Ray began to sob and cry and push me back. "It's

all your fault! It's all your fault! Why couldn't you just stay with the church?"

I cringed and tried again to explain and added, "While Dad's away you and I will have to milk the cows."

A neighbor came to assist in convincing Dad to go for help. Finally, he consented.

I watched from my spot on the porch as they rode away to the mental ward at Ephrata hospital.

* The family farm from the fields across the road

CHAPTER 14

Leaving Home

WE DID NOT SEE DAD FOR TWO VERY LONG WEEKS.

Meanwhile, peace was temporarily restored to the farmhouse while he was gone. My older brothers helped Aaron Ray and me with the farm work. When I found out Dad was coming home on Friday, we thought about a welcome-home gift for him. We decided to get him a little puppy since his dog had died earlier. I prepared Dad's favorite meal and purposed to put the past behind us. Dad was pleased to be back home again. When Aaron Ray and I showed him the little puppy, he smiled, saying "I'll call him Buster, after the new friend I made at the hospital."

With medication and counsel, Dad seemed much more relaxed. He changed into his work clothes and headed right out to the barn after supper. On Saturday, when I was cleaning my parlor, I looked up to see Dad at the door. He appeared a bit uncomfortable. He cleared his throat, then said gruffly, "I cannot tell you where to go to church, but as long as you are at home you must wear your head covering."

"Sure, I can do that, and thanks Dad." I was proud of Dad for having had the courage to say that.

The weeks that followed went better than the weeks before the hospitalization. Dad, however, would drift in and out of unhealthy communication whenever a church member came to visit him. I began to dread seeing black cars coming into the driveway.

Dad still carefully guarded the mailbox and the telephone. Mom and I kept our devotionals carefully hidden away from Dad's sight. As was my daily habit, after helping Mom with the breakfast dishes, I set my paints out on the kitchen table and began to work on a milk can I was painting for a farmer. Mom rested in a nearby rocking chair and read books aloud to me as I painted. We enjoyed this time together. She read books like *The Hiding Place* by Corrie Ten Boom and other true stories.

Around eleven o'clock that morning I saw the mailman arrive and watched Dad hurry to the mailbox. I watched as he slowly walked across the yard towards the house, reading the mail as he went. Suddenly he stopped and stood in the middle of the yard. I knew something had gone wrong when I saw his face. I put down my paintbrush and braced myself as he rushed across the remainder of the yard. He burst into the front door, his face beet red with violent anger.

"You!" He pointed in my face, "Get out, get out of this house right NOW!"

I backed up and gulped. "Can I get my clothes first?" I asked.

"No, get out NOW, and you can't have the car either!"

By now Mom was in tears, begging Dad to calm down. He was so uncontrollably upset that I knew I needed to get out of his sight before he physically hurt me. I weakly hurried through the parlor, grabbed my purse, and headed out the back door. As I began my walk down the road, my mind was in a swirl. "What could have possibly upset Dad so much? What did I do? Is it something I said? What do I do now?" I thought to myself.

I walked with tears streaming down my face. I loved Dad's farm. I couldn't look back. I decided to walk the two miles to my married brother's house. I began to pray. At that moment what felt like a glowing, liquid warmth that I describe as a divine assurance came into my heart and comforted me supernaturally. I knew then and there that things would work out all right and eventually be okay. I walked on and wiped the tears from my face.

When I arrived at my brother's house, his wife welcomed me inside and gave me a warm hug, and told me I could stay as long as I needed to. At the same time, she reprimanded me in an effort to correct the errors of my ways. I realized I didn't want to stay there, so I called my oldest sister. She quickly came to pick me up.

There I discovered the Bishop had been to her house too. Her family was experiencing the same excommunication and shunning that I did.

The stay at my sister's house was a very healing time for me emotionally. I didn't realize how the tension at home had affected me until after I left. Still, I felt bad for Mom. I wanted to be with her, to help shield her from Dad's verbal abuse. I found out later that the letter that had upset Dad so much was a kind and gracious "Thank you for visiting" letter from the church that I had visited the week before in an effort to find a new congregation. I had filled out their visitor's card, and in the prayer requests section of the card I wrote, "Please pray for my dad Aaron Zimmerman's salvation." This is what angered him so much.

I also found out Dad sold the Mustang. I felt like I had lost a friend.

I got a letter from Edna, the Old Order Mennonite artist, at whose house the painting parties I enjoyed so much were held.

"You are now on the high road (an expression we used for the "worldly" road) and we are still on the low road. We can no longer travel side by side," the letter read. I was no longer welcome to attend. I was disappointed, but I did not feel bitter about the excommunication and shunning, only sorry that these minor differences had separated us.

That winter, Cousin Lydia and I decided to visit her sister Mary in Canada. After our summer mission trip, Mary returned and committed to staying on for a year as a cook at the boarding school for Native youth at Stirland Lake, Ontario. We heard that a woodcutting crew of Mennonite youth was going there on a two-week mission to help at the school. We decided to see if we could tag along to help out and visit Mary. The crew gave us a ride along to Canada, and all went well until we drove across the border. As the night wore on and we drove further into Canada, the snow began to fall heavier and heavier. Slowly and carefully we drove through the desolate north woods. Several times we slid off the road but managed to push our way out of the ditch. Finally, we arrived at our destination late at night.

Mary was waiting for us. She was very happy to see us. We had lots to tell her. I told her about the excommunication and she realized her status as a church member in the horse and buggy church was jeopardized by her mission service in the north.

"Ach," she exclaimed, "Let's talk about God and what He is doing. Oh, by the way, why don't we go on a day of prayer and fasting in the hunter's cabin across the lake on my day off?"

"That sounds like a great plan!" Lydia and I readily agreed.

We helped Mary prepare meals for the school students and the wood-cutting crew. We talked about many things as we peeled potatoes and chopped onions. When we served the meal, I couldn't help but notice that one of the wood-cutting crew members was watching me. Oh dear, I thought, I need to let him know I'm not available. He needs to know that I'm engaged to be married!

The crew member's name was Nathaniel, and he began to seek me out whenever he had the chance. He was a tall, handsome, blonde gentleman, and he knew how to get a lady's attention. This was a new experience for me, but I let it go on for a bit because I was unsure of how to handle the situation.

The day dawned bright and clear on the morning of our planned outing. The snow-covered lake required us to use snowshoes to cross it. Nathaniel saw us out by the shed. He stopped to talk and offered to fasten my snowshoes. Then he leaned down to adjust my scarf, brushed my bangs aside, and smiled, "Have fun, I'll see you later."

I did not like the sense that came with the kind gesture. My flesh was tempted to enjoy the attention, but I realized I needed to put a stop to this.

We started across the lake with only our Bibles and water bottles. It took a bit of skill to learn how to walk in snowshoes, not to mention energy! Since we were fasting, we left without breakfast. My stomach began to growl even before we reached the halfway point where we paused for a break. I wrote in the snow the words "I love Ray."

"Come on let's keep moving," Mary urged. We plodded on, keeping our eyes on the distant shore, which gradually grew closer. By the time we reached the other shore, we were exhausted and famished!

"I think the cabin is over there," Mary gestured at a point in the tree line on the bank of the lake.

Just as she stepped off the ice, she broke through the crusted edge and plunged into the water up to her knees. We quickly grabbed her hand and pulled her onto the bank. We climbed the bank and entered the woods, but there was no sight of the cabin.

"Maybe it's this way," Mary said, leading us in yet another

direction. I was beginning to question the wisdom of our decision. What if Mary can't find the cabin? We needed to warm ourselves and Mary needed to dry out her boots and stockings.

"You guys stay here," Mary suggested. "I'm going deeper into the woods to look."

"No way," Lydia said, "We'd better stay together."

Together we crested a little knoll and spotted the cabin, nestled in among the pine forest... and what a welcome sight it was! We whooped and slapped Mary on the back.

"Good going Mary!" we congratulated her.

The hunter's cabin had a few crude bunk beds on two sides of the cabin and a corner fireplace. We gathered wood and built a fire. A dreadful smoke filled the room as we struggled to keep it lit. Finally, we got it burning well enough to warm the cabin. The warmth combined with our sore bodies made us so sleepy we collapsed onto the hard bunk beds and slept for hours. Sometime in the early afternoon, we awoke.

"Oh no!" Mary cried out, "The sky's clouded over. We better get out of here before it starts to snow." She reached for her boots and stockings, now dried and warmed by the fireplace. We doused the fire with water and fastened our snowshoes. By now I was so hungry I felt weak. We followed our tracks back across the lake. A north wind was now blowing and we got colder and colder as the temperature dropped.

"I need a break," I called to my cousins.

"We gotta keep moving," Mary replied rather sharply and anxiously.

So I pushed myself on. Snow began to fall gently at first but the heavier it fell, the whiter the atmosphere became, and the more difficult it was to find and follow our tracks. Silently I began to pray. By now my hands and feet felt numb with cold. We followed each other in a single file line. It was nearly dark when we finally reached the shores of Stirland Lake.

We dropped our snowshoes by the shed, then headed straight for the dining room pantry. We smuggled a bunch of food back to Mary's bedroom, where we broke our fast and feasted. We realized the trip had been stupid, but we were still determined to keep as much of our commitment as possible. So we prayed together until we fell into a deep sleep.

Nathaniel grew bolder in his advances toward me. At one point I told him I had a boyfriend, but that did not seem to deter him in the least. Finally, an idea came to me that felt like a "God idea."

"Can we meet somewhere private tomorrow?" I asked him. Then I added, "I have something I want to tell you."

He seemed very pleased by the request. We arranged a

time and place to meet.

Later I met him by the fence. He leaned in close, smiled sweetly, and asked, "How are you doing; what's on your mind?"

"Just fine," I replied.

I then proceeded to share my testimony. I told him how I was born again by faith in Christ's death on the cross for my sin. He straightened up and stepped back a bit, but I grew bolder with each sentence.

"I'm a new person now Nathaniel, I want to follow God's way and not self and sin." God empowers us to live a life of victory when we are filled with the Holy Spirit. I told him how I was baptized in the Holy Spirit and what an incredible difference it had made in my life.

He stepped back even more, then looked around as if he was trying to find a way of escape, but I stepped closer to him, saying, "You need to make a decision... who are you going to serve Nathaniel? Self and sin, or are you going to serve God?"

Somehow I knew all the while that there was a wrong spirit motivating him in his pursuit of me, and the power of God's Word would reveal his motives. Sure enough, he cleared his throat and said "That's interesting." Then he excused himself and walked away.

I contentedly smiled to myself. It worked! Then I prayed,

"Thank you Lord for protecting me." I prayed for Nathaniel too, that he would find the courage to come to Christ with his sin and find forgiveness and cleansing.

Nathaniel did not bother me for the remainder of the trip. I felt like I had won a great victory.

I was very glad to return home to Ray, my one and only sweetheart, and future husband.

In the spring, Ray and I began with wedding plans and preparations. We had our engagement pictures taken and sent out to family and friends to announce our engagement publicly.

Meanwhile, that summer my sister and I noticed many children in her neighborhood wandering the road with nothing to do. So we made up invitations and organized a backyard Bible club for them. This time I had a curriculum. We utilized the Good News Club program from the Child Evangelism Fellowship. We taught them Bible verses and songs and taught them how to pray. The club grew and the children became very dear to our hearts. As most of them were from broken homes, they had many emotional needs. We played games together in the backyard and had many fun outings together. On the last day of the club, we planned a special outing to the Strasburg Railroad and a picnic. Then we said goodbye to the children.

During this time of outreach, I began to notice I had a

desire for more biblical education. When Ray and I talked about it, he too expressed a similar desire. So we made plans to go to Bible school after our marriage. We chose Rhema Bible Training Center in Tulsa, Oklahoma, the same ministry that had blessed our lives so much through the teachings of the mini-books.

As the summer progressed, Mom called me at my sister's house and told me that Dad had consented to let me come home for the few months that remained until our marriage. I was glad to go home again; I missed the farm, my bedroom, and Aaron Ray. Things remained relatively peaceful between Dad and me that summer.

* The farm from the bridge down the road

CHAPTER 15

Wedding Bells

OCTOBER 8, 1988, WAS THE DAY WE HAD CHOSEN FOR OUR WEDDING.

Autumn was my favorite season of the year. Since I was no longer a member of the church, I was free to wear a white wedding gown made by my sister and carry a bouquet, both of which were forbidden in the church where my sisters were married. They were only allowed to wear light blue or lavender dresses. I chose a combination of my favorite flowers: red roses, white carnations, and daisies for my bouquet. Daisies were extra special to me since Ray often brought me a handful of freshly picked daisies to our dates.

On the morning of our wedding day, I determined to remain relaxed no matter what went right or what went wrong that day. I decided it was going to be a good day. My new friend Mandy came all the way from Canada to sing at our wedding.

My decision to "have a good day, no matter what" proved to be an important one. On my way up the backstairs of the church, my gown got caught on a nail. A baby cried all during the processional, but I hardly noticed as I focused on the blessings of the day. I was pleased with how Dad seemed to enjoy the day despite his disappointment that I did not get married in his church. For a wedding present, Ray's grandmother gave us a beautiful quilt, which she made herself. The gifts from my parents were half of a pig, a quarter beef, handmade quilts and comforters, and a used bedroom suite. They also gave us, a brand new, handcrafted kitchen table and chairs. We were blessed by many other meaningful gifts and well wishes from many relatives and friends.

We had decided our honeymoon destination would be to visit the Bible school we wanted to attend. On our way west, we stopped in Ohio to visit an air and space museum and the Gateway to the West in Missouri.

Before long we grew tired of eating out; we missed our mothers' home-cooked meals. When we arrived in Tulsa, we stayed at a Residence Inn, equipped with a small kitchen. For our first home-cooked meal, we decided on a vegetable, meat, and mashed potato dinner. I peeled and cooked the potatoes, but when I tried to remove the lid, it wouldn't budge! Ray, with his strong carpenter's arms, couldn't lift the lid either. We ended up having to call the maintenance man to come and help us! The suction had drawn the lid inward into the kettle.

"Well I'll be, I never saw the likes of this before." the maintenance man exclaimed as he pried and pounded the lid. Finally, the lid gave way. By now the potatoes had partly mashed on their own and our home-cooked meal was ready. Thus was my experience of presenting Ray with my first home-cooked meal.

When we stepped onto the campus of what is now called Rhema Bible Training College, we felt a sense of awe and a knowing came to our hearts that this was indeed the place for our next steps in life. This "knowing" confirmed what we felt in our hearts previously. We had a wonderful time exploring the campus, attending a class, and talking with the admissions personnel. We were relieved to discover the price was very affordable, though we decided it would be best if we worked a year at home to save money and prepare to pay the tuition and living costs in Tulsa.

On our way back East, we visited Gatlinburg, Tennessee,

where I got good pictures of the historic Pigeon Forge Mill. I painted that scene later, and it became one of the best sellers among my artwork.

In Tennessee, Ray wanted me to experience one of the sports he enjoyed in his teen years. We backpacked the Appalachian Trail for a day and one night. The fall foliage was breathtaking.

We went horseback riding (a sport I enjoyed since childhood), and in Virginia we visited a cave. Back in PA, we settled into our first home: a small trailer in the country at the edge of a cornfield near a creek. I loved the country surroundings of our new home.

The responsibility of housework and meals was a very easy transition for me since Mom had groomed me for this role. She taught me all the skills I would need for the task. It was fun to do the grocery shopping myself and pick a cereal other than Dad's favorite Cornflakes and Mom's healthy choice of Shredded Wheat. I tried out Golden Grahams and other sugary cereals, but I switched back to healthier choices when I discovered later that I had gained fifteen pounds that first year! What I enjoyed the most about my new home was the freedom I had to play my favorite Christian radio station without fear of Dad catching me listening to the radio. One of my favorite preachers on the radio was Dr. James Kennedy of Coral Ridge Presbyterian Church. I later discovered Dr. Dobson on his *Focus on the Family* radio broadcast, which equipped us in our marriage relationship and prepared us for future parenting. While washing dishes, I enjoyed listening to the *Radio Theater*, *Sugar Creek Gang*, and other *Audio Bookshelf Adventures*.

I freely placed my devotional materials from various ministries on my coffee table. I took a deep breath and realized our home would be a safe, relaxed, comfortable home.

Ray worked as a carpenter for his dad's business during the day. In the evening he began to study flight training manuals and worked towards his goal of a private pilot's rating.

These evenings of study and training were the first of the many sacrifices for the wife of a pilot. I had concerns about what that kind of career in aviation would mean for family life, but I did not express them to Ray. He was very excited and I did not want to get in the way of him fulfilling his dream.

That year I decided to conquer music theory. While I had learned basic notes and chords on my brother's guitar and instructional books, I wanted to be able to fluently read and improvise and learn to play the instrument better.

The old feeling of "you can't learn" reared its ugly head, which made me all the more determined to conquer yet another fear that tried to hold me back. I sought out a good teacher who was tough but kind. I practiced an hour each day and learned country gospel, classic, and blues. It was very rewarding to be able to read and play any style of music. So pleased was my teacher with my progress that after a year of lessons, he suggested I begin to teach beginners the concepts I had learned. So I made a poster announcing guitar lessons for the beginner student and hung the poster on a local hardware store bulletin board. Soon I began with a class of eight students and continued to teach guitar lessons for several years. Music is something Ray and I have always enjoyed together. He had learned to play the banjo in his teen years and we enjoyed singing and playing together on the weekends.

During that first year of marriage I continued to paint for the art dealer and various other commissions. We were very focused on saving as much money as we could to assist our move to Tulsa. Among my preparations for our move was an appointment for me to cut my hair and get a new wardrobe, which included purchasing a wedding ring. Rings were not worn in the culture we came from, but I did not want classmates to think that I was single and available.

I took this decision seriously and gave it a lot of thought. Up to this point, I continued to wear plain Mennonite clothes, even though we now belonged to a non-denominational church that did not require that of its members. I never had convictions that God required clothes to be a certain color or pattern, but I saw modesty taught very clearly in Scripture. I always desired to be modest.

My old friend from the Mennonite church came to see my new home. Near the end of our visit I said to her, "Kendra, I feel there is something I must tell you..."

I told her of my plans to cut my hair and no longer wear the Mennonite covering. I was a bit taken aback by her response, though not entirely surprised.

"Oh no please don't do that!" She cried and embraced me in a hug. Her tears fell on my shoulder as she begged me not to do that. "I don't want you to go to hell," She sobbed.

"Besides, how are people going to know that you are a Christian?" She wailed. Suddenly I realized how differently I saw things.

"I believe the Bible tells us it's by our love and by the fruits of the Holy Spirit, not our outward appearance," I answered. "Besides, looks can be very deceiving. Our actions and attitude reveal who we really are."

I watched her go out the door, feeling sad about how we parted and sad that she actually believed what she had just said. It served as a kind of final marker that we were once and for all leaving the life we once knew to go where God was directing us to go.

CHAPTER 16

Rhema Days

IN THE LATE SUMMER OF 1989, WE PACKED ONLY THE ESSENTIALS NEEDED FOR OUR STAY IN TULSA.

We put them all in an enclosed 5x7 foot trailer Ray built for our move west. We said our goodbyes to our family and friends, feeling very excited about this new adventure.

When we arrived in Tulsa we checked into a cheap motel near the school, then drove around town looking for an apartment to rent. The next day we found one several blocks from the school with the cost of $300.00 per month for rent.

The meaning of the word "rhema" described our experience in Bible school so well. In the New Testament, there are two Greek words used to identify words from God. They are "logos" and "rhema." Logos is used in 1 John 1:1, which states, "In the beginning was the (logos) Word, and the Word was with God," referring to the written Word of God and to Jesus himself, who is the living Word. Rhema is the spoken word of God as it appears in Ephesians 6:17, which tells us to, "... take the sword of the Spirit, which is the (rhema) word of God."

The written word of God became our foundation and the spoken word our direction as it was quickened to our understanding by the Holy Spirit, becoming "rhema" words to us. Day after day, class after class the Scriptures were opened to our hearts ever so clearly. Previously, Bible interpretation was a mystery to me, but here at school we were taught how to let the Bible interpret itself by studying the context, asking questions such as, "Who was the intended audience?" and "What does this mean in light of the surrounding verses?" Then finally, we were exhorted to never make a doctrine out of obscure passages of Scripture. Some teachings were meant for a particular time and place, while others were universal applications for all times. I began to realize that a lack of proper Biblical interpretation is the cause of the many divisions and differences within

Christian churches.

In our first year, we studied the Old and New Testaments, the foundational doctrines of Christ, and church history. In church history class, I had to pick a denomination and write an essay about its history. It had to be typed - which was a problem. I'd never used a typewriter before in my life, nor was I ever assigned to write a report or an assay in the one-room school. I found a cheap old typewriter at a garage sale and plunked away on the keys, one at a time! I chose to study the history of the Mennonite Church. It was a very enriching experience to learn their roots in the time of the Reformation. I gained insight into their belief system today. I also realized that to know our history is to know ourselves better. It was in this homework assignment that I gained much of the material I wrote in the first chapter of this book.

We quickly bonded with other classmates from around the world. Our favorite way of getting acquainted was to ask each other, "So, how did you come to know the Lord?" We heard many touching testimonies of changed lives. Decades later, many of these classmates are among my closest and dearest friends.

I quickly realized the beauty and blessing of true spiritual unity, no matter the racial or cultural background. Christ's Spirit makes us family. This unity possessed a deep richness that I had not known before. I was in awe of that reality. Previously I was taught that the unity of the faith was adhering to the doctrine of the Mennonite faith; dressing the same way and doing things the same way. I used to wonder, "Could one be a wholehearted follower of Christ and not be Mennonite?" I asked my new friends and classmates lots of questions. I was amazed by how they had come from far and wide; one from Switzerland, another from India. Karen was from Arizona. Her parents split up when she was ten years old, which eventually culminated in an ugly divorce that left her vulnerable as a victim of molestation when she was kidnapped by a family member soon after. But when she came to Christ, He gloriously redeemed her life. She married and had a beautiful family of her own. Karen and her husband felt called to be pastors, and they wanted to help train families to be healthy and strong. She asked me many questions about my background. We were fascinated by our different upbringings and yet how we both valued homemaking so much. She liked to quilt and sew and preserve her garden vegetables. I'd jokingly ask her, "Karen, are you sure you're not Mennonite?"

Another friend we made had never met a Mennonite or an Amish person. She had heard about them, but she assumed they were a cult of some kind. Because of the dark clothes they wore, she associated them with warlocks or some other satanic group!

It was early in our first year that we began looking for jobs in earnest. Ray had many valuable skills, having had so much experience building houses with his father since he was fifteen years old, but no carpenter crew was hiring any part-time workers. Ray finally took a job cleaning offices for Florafax. I never heard him complain about the demotion or the $4.00 an-hour salary. He whistled on his way out the door every afternoon and looked forward to his half-hour of flying once a week on Sunday mornings before church (that was all our budget could afford). Eventually, he decided to put his flight training on hold until we finished Bible school and only flew enough to stay current. This was a lean time for us financially, yet we knew we were right where we needed to be; therefore we knew God would provide. How? We weren't always sure. I'd take the $20.00 bill designated for groceries and a calculator each week to the warehouse markets and make a fun game out of how much I could get with so little. I would find some pretty amazing bargains, and somehow the $20.00 always reached!

One particularly challenging month before we found steady work, we noticed a business van parked in the parking lot of our apartment complex. Ray called the number on the side of the van. As it turned out, the vehicle had been stolen from the company. They were so pleased that we had called them that they gave us a large reward which covered our cost of tuition for that month! Several months later, the school announced that students from the state of PA were meeting for breakfast at Shoney's. The restaurant had a large, beautiful, all-you-can-eat breakfast buffet, but since we did have extra money to eat out, we decided to go anyway to meet with classmates and perhaps only buy the smallest item on the menu: one egg and a piece of toast. It was a bit painful to smell the delicious smells coming from the buffet as we made that decision. Just when the waitress came to our side of the table, a distinguished gentleman approached us, knelt by our chair, and whispered, "The Lord told me to buy your breakfast. Please order all you can eat!" We were astonished and very grateful. We thanked him heartily and told the waitress, "We'll take the breakfast buffet." The only other time we ate out that year was on our first wedding anniversary. Ray's mother sent us a lovely card with a money gift and wrote that we were to treat ourselves and go out to eat.

Looking for a job was a frightening challenge for me since I never had to work outside the home before. I applied at various restaurants and stores, but it seemed no one wanted to hire me. I wondered if it had anything to do with the fact that I did not have a high school education. I decided then that the first chance I had I would earn a GED.

One afternoon I was sitting in the office at Sam's Club

trying to fill out the application, but I struggled to understand the questions. Finally, I excused myself and went out to the car and cried. I did not want a job outside the home; I wanted to paint! But I had to make money somehow. I never returned to Sam's Club to finish the process. Instead, I visited a small room at school that was called the "Job Room." There on the wall hung a poster with a long list of help-wanted ads. Again tears of frustration filled my eyes as my finger ran down the list. None of the jobs interested me. I could no longer read, so blurred was my vision from the tears running down my face, so I just picked a number at random. At home, I called the number. A sweet voice answered the phone, and she agreed to meet with me right away. I was pleased to discover the voice on the other end belonged to an elderly lady looking for someone to keep up with her housework as she cared for her sickly husband.

On my first day, Christine and I got acquainted over a cup of cold lemonade. I was eager to get started, but she was in no hurry. I realized later she mostly wanted someone around for companionship. Each afternoon when I arrived she wanted to sit first and have tea and devotions, and then perhaps go for a nice walk. This job suited me very well, although sometimes I felt guilty for getting paid for such an easy task, which looked like something of a lady's maid. I painted her nails and hung her church clothes back in the closet. She belonged to the Methodist church and she still kept up the tradition of wearing hats to church. Christine had lots of pretty hats of all styles and colors. My job was to put the hat in its proper box with the same color shoes and put them back in the closet.

She called me her "Hutterite friend." I had to educate her concerning the difference between Amish, Mennonites, Quakers, and Hutterites!

She invited me along to her many club meetings. At a book club, I met her friend Ellen. As it turned out, Ellen's husband, Tom Davies, was a carpenter by trade and was looking to retire soon. Ray and I arranged to meet with Tom right away.

Tom took a liking to Ray immediately and gave him a deck repair job at the home of a banker in a wealthy housing development by Keystone Lake. Ray was so pleased with this open door. Finally, he was able to quit his cleaning job and get a decent salary. Ray's new job by the lake was pleasant and prosperous. I helped out on occasion when he needed an extra hand to hold the support posts for the deck framing. Many of the owners of the houses by the lake were wealthy businessmen. They would come home from their office jobs and stand by, with cold drinks in their hands, and chat while watching Ray work. They were amazed by his efficiency. Word spread that he was a trustworthy and conscientious worker. The jobs began to line up and fill the year with renovations at each of their homes. The psychologist next door asked if I could come to his house to clean. He also wanted me to be there when his three children came home from school, make dinner, and make homemade cookies for them. I accepted the job but continued to help Christine as well.

* Ray building decks by Keystone Lake

CHAPTER 17

Where Circumstances and Destiny Meet

"HOW OLD ARE YOU?" I ASKED CHRISTINE ONE DAY.

"I don't know," she replied.

"When is your birthday?" I tried again.

"I don't know that either," She said. Then she laughed at my perplexed expression and in her southern accent said, "Sit down here, I'm going to tell you a story. I was born in the country as a very sick baby. My poor mother couldn't care for me proper-like so she sent me with the peddler to find a home for me. A farm family took me in. They had a large family of their own. They treated their own children well, but they did not take good care of me. As soon I was able they sent me out to pick cotton and hoe corn in the fields. They treated me as their slave. They bought shoes for the other children but not for me.

"One Sunday, a neighbor took me to Sunday school with them and that is where I got my first Bible. But when I returned home, the man of the house grabbed the Bible from my hands and threw it in the wood stove. I went to bed and cried. I decided I would run away the first chance I could get. That chance came when the family went to the house for dinner before me. Since I was not finished with my row of onions, I kept hoeing. As soon as they disappeared, I ran across the fields towards town."

"Were you scared?" I asked, amazed at her unusual backstory.

"Oh yes," she replied, "but I remembered from Sunday school the story about Moses' exit from Egypt, and crossing the Red Sea on dry land. So I prayed, 'Lord God if you can help Moses cross the Red Sea, I know you can help me find a home!' When I arrived in town I went into the town square. Those were the days when everyone came to town in their horse and buggy or wagon. I went to the public facility where the ladies would go to wash their faces to freshen up from the dusty ride into town. I sat in a chair and waited.

"By now I was very hungry. Soon a well-dressed lady came in with crying twins in her arms. I jumped up and offered to help with the babies. The lady was very grateful for my help. I asked her if I could work for her. I told her that I was good with babies and that I could help her with the twins. The lady looked at my dirty ragged clothes and bare feet and took pity on me. As it turns out, she was a wealthy doctor's wife. They took me in and treated me as their own daughter. They bought me new clothes and treated me very well. Most of all, they took me to church. So, that is how God helped me find a new home." She finished with a smile.

I marveled at her story. "So you really do not know how old you are!?" I asked.

"I'm guessing I'm eighty years old," She shrugged.

Christine and I grew to enjoy each other's company. However, unbeknownst to me, her daughter Kathryn, who lived next door, was growing very jealous. I kept my distance when Kathryn came to visit her mother. She was a very toxic person. She was an ex-pastor's wife, now divorced; a "battle axe" embittered at the church, God, and the whole world.

She controlled and manipulated her mother. Christine went along with everything for the sake of peace.

I listened to a conversation between Kathryn and her mother as I dusted the furniture in the living room.

"Please Kathryn, won't you go with me to the Mother and Daughter Banquet at church, just this once?"

Kathryn let loose a long line of choice words about the church and its hypocrisies, then stormed out the front door. Christine turned to me and asked, "Will you go with me to the banquet?"

"Oh, I'd love to," I replied. "I've never been to a mother and daughter banquet before!"

This made it extra fun for Christine. She took me by the hand and walked me around the banquet hall and introduced me to all her friends.

"This is Elva Hurst my Hutterite friend all the way from Lancaster County, PA." She gloated, still holding my hand.

Since I still had a bit of a Mennonite look about me, they treated me as if I only had a fourth-grade education and could only speak Dutch. They spoke to me in plain and simple terms. I was amused. Finally, we sat at an extravagantly decorated table with party favors and flowers everywhere. After an amazing full-course dinner, we sat back and were entertained by the Tulsa Triune Sisters, singing silly songs in 50's music style about the life of a mother with six daughters, "I wish I were dripping with pearls but instead I'm dripping with girls!"

When we returned from our delightful evening, I immediately sensed that the brewing storm next door was building into a hurricane!

We finished our first year at Rhema in May, then decided to move home for the summer and work hard for three months to save money so we could pay for our final year in Bible school. Christine begged me to come back in the fall.

"In fact," she said, "could you house-sit for me while I tour Scotland for the month of September?"

I promised her that we would be glad to do that. We also decided that when we returned, we would move into an apartment complex not far from Christine's house. We put in our name and we were assured an apartment would be ready for us in early October. This would work out well, we figured.

Christine called me several times that summer. She told me the news that her husband had passed away and told me all about the funeral.

"I'm really looking forward to your return," she said during one of our final phone calls before we headed back for the fall.

We had a profitable summer. I painted for the art dealer and Ray worked for his dad.

The last week of August, we again packed our few pieces of furniture, ironing board, and home-canned fruits and vegetables into the trailer and headed back West. When we arrived at Christine's home, the key was right where she told us it would be, along with a note reminding us not to forget to water the houseplants, to be extra careful when I dusted her angel collection, and to be sure to lock up at night. We settled in quickly and started school. Within the first week however, Kathryn started to make trouble. She'd come in the front door without knocking and scurry around and water the houseplants that I had just watered. Then she sat and watched TV in the living room, turning it up loudly after we went to bed. After several nights of this, Ray politely asked her not to come in after the doors were locked for the night. She stuck her nose in the air and smirked, saying, "I can come into my mother's house any ol' time I want to."

At four o'clock the next morning, we heard the garage door open and the car rev loudly in the garage. Ray dressed and hurried to see if someone was stealing Christine's car.

It was Kathryn.

"I need to take mom's car to the garage," She called as she drove out the drive.

"At four in the morning? I don't think so!" Ray concluded, "This woman is trying to make life miserable for us on purpose and I'm not going to put up with it!"

"But we need to stay; we promised Christine we would stay," I insisted.

At work the next day Ray told Tom Davies about Kathryn's actions.

"Yes, she's a mean one," Tom said. "You better come stay with us until your apartment is ready. We have a comfortable, spacious, prophet's room with a bathroom and refrigerator where you can stay until your apartment is ready."

Meanwhile, Kathryn acted more and more irrationally. She knew I liked antiques. She gathered up all of Christine's antiques and locked them in the spare bedroom.

That Saturday morning we packed up and moved the trailer to Tom and Ellen's house.

Ellen greeted us, assuring us over and over, "It's not your fault, we are glad to have you here."

I continued to clean Ellen's large ranch house; we enjoyed each other's company. On Saturday nights, the four of us ate ice cream and watched old cowboy movies together. Tom had a horse and a small stable in the fenced-in backyard.

"Ginger needs exercise. Ride her as often as you wish," Tom told me. I rode Ginger regularly in a large vacant lot that was all grown over in prairie grass.

I was eager for Christine's return so we could iron out the situation. I called her on the day of her return but she refused to talk to me. She called me a traitor.

"I trusted you with my house, and you didn't keep your

word," she accused. I cringed as I tried to explain, but the line went dead.

I couldn't believe it. I'd never been called a traitor before. I felt very misunderstood and wrongly accused!

I tried to visit her at her home, but when she peeped through the window and saw who it was, she quickly locked the door. We figured Kathryn had told her a pack of lies about us. Who knows for sure? I knelt beside my bed and prayed often, "Lord help me mend this relationship."

Over the coming weeks, I tried a few more times. On the day we celebrated her birthday last year, I decorated a cake and put it on her front steps. I put a gift certificate and a note as a peace offering on Kathryn's front door as well. But my gestures for reconciliation were not reciprocated.

Tom and Ellen told us later that they always had a delicate relationship with Christine and her daughter.

The Bible teaches us that, "As much as depends on us, to live peaceably with all men." Tom reminded me, "You did your part, let it go at that. For now, there is nothing more you can do."

I just wanted to fix the situation quickly and get back to where I had been in my relationship with Christine. It took faith to let it go.

I enjoyed my weekly outings with Ginger and cantered blissfully into the wind out across the fields.

Ginger was a city horse. When I rode her on the road, even with all kinds of loud cars passing by, she stayed calm. However, out in the prairie, she was skittish. I had to pay close attention to her ears. She'd lay her ears back and leap sideways when a rabbit ran from the bushes, and she jumped at the slightest noise.

One beautiful Saturday morning, we galloped across the fields. Suddenly, a gunshot sounded nearby. She reared, then put her head down and raced towards home. I quickly lost control of her. I couldn't get her head back up. She leaped over the ditch and onto the road, heading straight into the traffic. Cars turned aside for us as I hung onto the saddle horn, but I was losing my hold. Just as Ginger briefly swerved off the edge of the road, I tumbled into the grass. I remember seeing hooves fly by me and thinking, "I'm still alive!"

A lady jumped from a car nearby and rushed to my side. "Are you okay?!" She called out to me.

I asked if she could get me to the horses' home. I was in pain but was able to walk. With her help, I limped to the car. When we arrived at Ellen's house, Ginger was contentedly eating grass in the backyard. Now I felt betrayed by Ginger too. Ellen met us at the door and put me in a hot bath.

"Where does it hurt? I'll take you to our doctor." She fussed and brought me a cold glass of sparkling grape juice on ice. I slowly sipped the liquid. I didn't know there was such a thing as sparkling fruit juice; I enjoyed the luxury.

A visit to the doctor confirmed that I had a sprained knee and ankle. I would have to go back to school on crutches for a while. Otherwise, I was okay, except I had broken my glasses and now, unfortunately, I feared riding horses. Tom instructed that the remedy was to get back on the horse as soon as I was able.

This time I only rode her inside the corral for a while, and then only on the road where nothing ever fazed her. I did not ride her in the wilds of the prairie ever again!

For our second year at Bible school, we had to choose what area of ministry we felt called to serve in.

We didn't feel any particular leading to train in the evangelist, pastoral, missionary, teacher, or ministers of music fields, but since I was involved in the children's ministry at the school's church, I chose the children's group and Ray choose the ministry of helps.

I was educated in the Biblical physiology of learning and how to conduct Sunday school and teach children using flannel graphs, visual aids of all kinds, and of course, puppets. I was fascinated by the many tools available for learning that I had never experienced in my childhood.

That year I had to learn how to write and preach a sermon. I studied homiletics, which is the art and science of preaching. I wrote and rewrote my sermon, then practiced on my classmates, not realizing I would soon be putting these tools into practice with a discovery I was soon about to make.

By now we had moved from Tom and Ellen's spare room into our own apartment, but I continued to do housecleaning for Ellen. After school, I helped her clean out the large walk-in closet in the prophet's room where Ray and I had stayed earlier. We sat together on the bed while looking through some old books when Ellen reached into a box and pulled out a classic written by William Allen Bixler titled *Chalk Talk Made Easy.* Immediately I was drawn to the old book. It was so old it smelled funny. Slowly and carefully, I turned the fragile pages of the book and looked at the exercises and illustrations.

"You can have it if you think you can use it," Ellen offered.

Back at the apartment that evening, I read through the old treasure and realized I could use this as a teaching tool for my Sunday school classes. I didn't know anything about this old art form but learned that chalk talk was a tool used in the 1800s and early 1900s by pastors and teachers to illustrate their lessons and sermons. Chalk talk was used extensively on the mission field to communicate the Gospel. I read about famous chalk artists from the past like Phil Saint, Karl Steele, and Esther Frye.

I could hardly wait until Sunday to give chalk talk a try in the classroom. I read in the book how the artist drew in chalk or crayon and talked at the same time.

"Oh my," I thought, "that would take a lot of concentration to do them both simultaneously!"

Suddenly I had an Idea. I took my old cassette recorder into the bathroom to avoid the sound of the nearby airport and its constant noise of planes taking off and landing. I settled on the closed toilet lid and pressed the record button. On my guitar, I played and sang a children's Sunday school song. Then I picked up the Sunday school lesson and read the Bible story and taught the lesson. Midway through my recording, the neighbor upstairs flushed his toilet and the water gushed noisily down the pipes.

"Oh dear," I thought to myself. I didn't want that sound effect! So I started over and redid the whole recording. Then I taped a piece of Canson pastel paper to the refrigerator, pressed play, and practiced my very first chalk talk. It was the story in the book of Matthew about the rich man who built bigger barns to store his wealth, but he was not rich towards God. In the scene, I drew a small barn and a bigger barn surrounded by shocks of wheat. It was a simple but colorful harvest picture. I practiced it a few more times before Sunday.

Finally, my Sunday came around. My class of 50 first

graders sat quietly and listened as they intently watched me draw. I marveled at their attentiveness, as previously it was always a struggle to get and hold their attention. Supposedly we only remember approximately 10% of what we read and 20% of what we hear, but we remember 50% of what we see and hear. I was so pleased with myself and realized, if that saying was true, then this would be a very effective way to drive the lesson into their little hearts and minds.

* *Practicing one of my first chalk talks*

* *Divine discovery in Ellen's closet*

CHAPTER 18

A Surprise Gift

ONE NIGHT AFTER SUPPER, THERE WAS A KNOCK ON OUR DOOR.

It was Tom Ivanusa, our good friend and classmate, carrying a big box in his arms.

"Surprise, I brought you a present!" He grinned broadly.

We opened the box and discovered a brand-new TV.

"I won it at work," Tom quickly explained. "I already have a nice TV at home and I thought I'd give this one to you guys."

Our classmates noticed we didn't own a TV, and they couldn't understand how we could live without one. Since

Ray and I both grew up without TV, we didn't think we were missing anything.

I had mixed feelings about the gift as I had heard that there were many negative things on the airways. I wasn't sure I wanted that influence in our home. With no antenna, we were limited to local stations only. We made the decision to not connect to cable TV, which helped us to control the many things that came with cable television. We managed to keep tight control of the box. I could never work TV into a daily habit; it felt too much like wasting valuable time. Later in life, when folks asked how in the world I could accomplish so much, I'd often reply, "I don't watch TV every day!"

Despite my initial reservations, I eventually discovered the famous artist Bob Ross and his show *The Joy of Painting*. I was mesmerized by his "wet on wet" technique and carefully watched each stroke of his brush. Furthermore, his calm and confident manner made me feel like I could paint oil on canvas too! Inspired by his confidence, I went to Walmart and bought Bob Ross brand oil paints, canvases, and of course, a palette knife with which I learned how to texture my paintings of mountains and trees, just like Bob Ross did.

Previously I had always painted on stones, slates, and other inexpensive inferior surfaces. Using real oils on real canvas was special, and for the first time, I truly felt like a bonafide artist!

I learned from Bob Ross many valuable lessons in color, composition, and perspective. I became aware, years later, that I unconsciously combined Bob Ross' speed painting technique with the 19th-century chalk art that in turn evolved into the chalk talk presentations that I do today.

Between studies and cleaning homes, I found time to practice painting oil on canvas Bob Ross-style. The drying canvases lined the walls of our apartment.

When we graduated from our second and final year in Tulsa we were so pleased to receive our diplomas. Since our families were too far away to celebrate with us, Tom and Ellen sat in the audience to cheer for us. Afterwards, they took us to an ice cream shop to celebrate our accomplishment.

"Now," Ellen said, "we are going to our house to take pictures of you and Ray in your caps and gowns."

I hadn't thought of taking pictures of us in our getup and appreciated the kind gesture.

After we had finished taking pictures, Tom reached into his wallet and drew out a $20.00 bill, and said, "Here, this is seed money for your dream farm. Someday we will come to Pennsylvania to see it." We were deeply touched. They understood our desire to raise our family on a farm and believed it could happen.

We hugged Tom and Ellen and said goodbye one last

time. A lump came into my throat; they had become like family to us and meant so much to us.

The gang at Keystone Lake threw a very elaborate farewell party for us. With wrapped gifts and a large, lovely decorated cake, and lots of food. We were amazed. Then we realized they were up to something. They sat around us in the living room of the banker's home. In passionate tones, they expressed their appreciation for the quality work we had done on their homes.

"But there is much more that could be done!" They said. "Would you please consider staying to continue to help us work on our homes?" The wives turned to me and offered a pay raise to continue to clean their houses.

"We have a rental property you can live in," they offered. We gratefully listened but hesitated to give a definite answer.

Then as if to convince us, one of the gentlemen spoke up, "I heard you came to Tulsa to go to Bible college, so if you were planning to start a church you could use the clubhouse right here at Keystone Lake."

They were so kind to offer all that to us, but we quickly explained our desire to return home to Lancaster County, which had been our original plan.

After returning to Lititz, PA we rented a farmhouse apartment. We placed the farm seed money from Tom and Ellen in a box and tucked it away in the desk drawer.

After purchasing appliances for the apartment we only had $48.00 left to our name! Fortunately, a relative welcomed us home with groceries that lasted until Ray got his first paycheck from his carpentry job with his father.

* Graduating class of 1991

CHAPTER 19

Finally Found A Place We Could Afford!

FOR FIVE WONDERFUL YEARS, WE LIVED COMFORTABLY IN OUR LOVELY RUSTIC FARMHOUSE APARTMENT

at the Raymond Wenger Farm on Sleepy Hollow Road. During the first year, Ray and I both studied and earned our GED. I found I struggled to understand algebra concepts. Math had a way of reducing me to tears, even though Ray tried to help explain it to me. Thanks to multiple choice answers, I was able to slide by math. I was however fascinated by my language arts textbook. I took many notes and filed them away for future reference. When I wrote an essay, the instructor was so pleased with the piece, it earned special attention. She even entered it into a writer's competition!

Later on, I got involved in the children's ministry at a large local congregation and continued to use the chalk talk technique in Sunday school. We were offered a position at the church as assistants to the children's pastor. We felt honored but declined the offer. While we sensed some kind of a call to ministry, we knew that was not what it was. The pastors offered us another place of service on the visitation team; again we declined.

One Sunday a few months later I was doing a chalk talk in my sixth-grade Sunday school class. The children's pastor was observing and asked me to do a chalk talk for the entire children's congregation the following Sunday. It just so happened that the morning I performed a church worker from Hosanna Christian Fellowship was there observing our children's ministry program. She approached me afterward and asked me if I would do a chalk talk for their children's church. I felt since it was children's ministry, it was still within my comfort zone, so I accepted the invitation.

I was no longer comfortable using my homemade recordings as the soundtrack, so I began to have my stories professionally recorded at Rissler Music Services, a recording studio owned by a relative. I followed the same format that combined songs, stories, and occasionally sound effects.

I told Ray I was going to need a real easel for this special presentation. I checked in various art stores for something that would suit my needs, but no easels were large or sturdy enough to hold the large gray bogus paper I used for this large-scale art. Ray decided to take me to his dad's workshop, and there we designed and built from scrap metal my very first chalk talk easel, complete with a light hood to light up the painting and a piece of spouting for the chalk tray! We set it up and then stood back to admire it.

Ray's dad appeared in the doorway and asked skeptically, "You're going to do what with that?" Still, I was pleased and couldn't wait to try it out.

The presentation for Hosanna Christian Fellowship was a success. The invitations come slowly at first and few and far in between, but things changed while I was doing a chalk talk for The Religious Release Time program for our local public school children at Brunnerville United Methodist Church in Lititz. There, Pastor Landis observed the chalk talk.

Afterward, he asked, "What are you doing this evening? Could you do a chalk talk for the Warwick Ministers Association Christmas Banquet tonight?"

"I'd be glad to," I replied, "however I do not have any adult programs."

"Oh that's quite alright," He answered. "I would just like

for the ministers to see what you could do for their church children's programs."

I agreed to come. The banquet was held at Chimney Corner Restaurant in Lititz. Since the banquet room was in the back end of the building, I had to lug my big, boxy easel case on wheels through the dining room.

"Who ya got in there?" a guest jokingly called out as I passed by. I blushed, suddenly feeling self-conscious about my homemade coffin-like box on wheels.

The chalk talk at the banquet was very well received. Many of the churches represented by the ministers invited me to their churches. Word of my work began to spread quickly and even extended into community service clubs of all kinds. The local Lions Club asked me to do a chalk talk for their district convention. They wanted the program to include their history and all the work they did in Lionism.

I did not have a personal computer, so I went to a friend's house from church and there she taught me how to do research and print out the materials from the internet that I would need to develop the program.

I commissioned another church friend to write an original song for this special recording.

I designed and practiced the picture in our basement while I was pregnant with our first child and dealing with morning sickness. Over and over I drew their emblem of a

Lion's roar in a sign that greets you as you enter the town in my painting. For a long time thereafter I'd get nauseous just seeing the Lion's head emblem on any town sign!

The hard work paid off well. The Lions Club members were so pleased with the program that their governors spread the word. For years I went from town to town, club to club, entertaining these patriotic service-minded citizens. Eventually, invitations came from Rotary clubs, Kiwanis, and the town women's clubs meetings as well.

It was in these community service club meetings that I learned, for the first time, to pledge allegiance to the flag of the United States of America. I learned patriotism from them as they sang together our great American patriotic songs.

The chalk talks thrust me into the public speaking arena; something for which I still felt inexperienced, so I sought help from the public library and checked out a book called *Speaking Secrets for the Masters*. I took notes with paper and pencil and studied the art of public speaking. The rules advised to "be yourself," "don't talk about something you know nothing about," and finally, "talk from the heart." I took the advice seriously, especially the admonition to speak from the heart, which I found made public speaking easier and much more enjoyable.

I had learned many valuable art lessons from trial and error, but an opportunity for further learning came in 1994 when a children's worker gave me the name of an elderly chalk artist near Pittsburgh, PA named Gary Means. I called him and he invited me to a chalk art workshop held at his church that coming fall.

It was over a four-hour drive to Mars, PA. It wasn't that far, but I was six months pregnant, so I asked Ray if he would take me to the workshop.

"I'm so sorry but I can't go," he said. "I have a cross-country training flight that weekend. But you go ahead and attend the workshop anyway." He encouraged.

I felt the need to go, but I really didn't want to drive alone. These were the days before GPS and cell phones, so Ray hand-wrote the directions for me and showed me on a map where I was going. Navigation is not one of my gifts. I turned the map around trying to figure out which way was west. I was timid about driving the turnpike by myself. I forced myself to face up to the challenge and decided to do the drive myself.

After a few wrong turns, I arrived just in time for the evening session. It was glorious to be surrounded by two dozen chalk artists from various states. I made new friends and gathered lots of helpful information on how to conduct chalk talks using blacklight artistry. Up to that, point my chalk talks were performed without fluorescent chalk and blacklight effects.

That night I checked into the cheapest motel in town. The walls were so thin I could hear the person in the next room snoring. I tossed and turned trying to get to sleep. At 2 a.m. I heard another person's alarm clock. I didn't get a wink of sleep that night. I sat, sleepy-eyed but excited, through two more sessions. By evening I was very weary. Outside, a steady rain began to fall turning into a pouring downfall that followed me the whole way home to Lancaster.

The next morning on our way to church my car tire went flat. As Ray pulled over to change the tire, I whispered a prayer of gratitude to God for watching out for me on my way home on the wet highways the night before!

March 10th, 1995 our first son Josiah was born. I was awed at the realization that while I had accomplished many things, motherhood was by far the most fulfilling! I scaled back the painting business and dismissed the guitar students to concentrate on this exciting new venture. I continued to do chalk talks on occasion, adding one new program to my lineup of offerings each year. This provided me with the perfect little "get out of the house" outing that every mother needs on occasion. All the while, we dreamed of living on a small farm of our own. The dream seemed far-fetched in reality, but very strong and real in our hearts.

One Sunday, on our way home from church, we noticed an old dilapidated farm down a long lane on Brunnerville

Road in Lititz.

When Josiah was just several months old Ray came home with news.

"I stopped at that farm after work today," he said. My ears perked up.

"Really?" I asked. "What did you find out about the place?"

The farm was established in 1859. The most recent owner had inherited the farm but never lived there. Thus, renters came and went for many years but they did not take care of the property very well.

Ray informed me the renter had given him the owner's contact information. That evening, he called Mr. Bomberger.

"I've just been thinking, I ought to sell the place," Bomberger commented. "I'm getting older and will be going to the nursing home soon."

"We think we'd like to buy the place. How much do you want for it?" Ray asked.

The owner explained he needed to give the Amish man who farmed the land the first chance. Meanwhile, we sought out a realtor friend from our church and asked about the possible likelihood of us buying this 91-acre farm. He put a plan into action to sell four two-acre lots out by the road. He would become the "buyer broker." Then, at settlement, we would only have to purchase and settle on our 20 acres.

The Amish man's offer did not suit the owner so we were

next in line to buy.

The events of the purchase fell into place and suddenly we became the owners of our very own farm.

We quickly discovered the farmhouse was unlivable. We spent our evenings painting the smoke-stained walls and cleaning rooms filled with junk and trash. We pulled twenty old appliances from the basement and attic that the previous renters had not bothered to haul away.

Vines had grown up the side of the house and into a broken upstairs window. The vine continued around the room's interior and grew up and out the chimney!

On a cold, crisp, snowy winter evening after supper, I went to help Ray finish preparing the house for moving day. Because of the snow and ice, I had to park our minivan at the end of the lane. I bundled up the baby and walked down the tree-lined lane on the snowy, moonlit night. The light of the moon cast shadows of tree branch patterns across my path. Up ahead, I could see smoke curl peacefully from the chimney into the night sky. Warm light spilled from the farmhouse windows onto the snow.

"It's my farm," I whispered to myself. I must give it a name. I pictured what the trees would look like in the summertime and decided to call it Shady Lane Farm. Excited by the name, I burst in the front door and called to Ray, "Hey, I have a name for the farm, let's call it Shady Lane Farm!"

"That describes it well!" He agreed to the name.

We heated the house with the wood from the fallen trees in the woods surrounding our property. As soon as spring arrived I purchased six laying hens. I eagerly anticipated taking my toddler and a basket on daily egg-hunting outings. Alas, on one morning visit to the hen house, all that remained was six heads! Raccoons got in during the night and ate the hens. I decided then and there I would not be bested by a bunch of varmints! I realized I needed proper fencing. After Ray helped me build a higher fence in another area I purchased more hens to try again.

One morning while flipping pancakes for breakfast, I happened to glance out the window just in time to see a hawk swoop down, grab, and fly off with a hen.

"So that's what's been happening to my chickens!" I hissed with fury.

That first year, before we cleared the briars and brush from the pasture, it was not uncommon to see pheasants walk by the house and coons come and go in broad daylight on their way to the creek. At night we heard the shrieking screams of a gray fox in the fields.

Rolling up our sleeves we began our homesteading, poor as peasants, yet feeling rich as kings for the privilege of having our very own place. We cleared the land and planted the crops. They did very poorly at first since the soil was so neglected and nutritionally unbalanced.

I eventually planted a branch from Dad's weeping willow tree, a sprout of Mom's lilac bush, a large garden, and a grape arbor. My dad took great interest in our farm. He helped us find our first tractor, an Allis-Chalmers 160 with a loader that served us well for many years.

That year, Tom and Ellen drove east to PA to visit us and see our farm. They were so pleased and proud and rejoiced with us.

Bethany Joy was born on January 26, 1998, and three years later Cora Anne arrived on the same day.

We did a lot of living on the farm. As soon as the girls were old enough, we had tea parties under the weeping willow tree with their friends and grandmothers. In the summertime, I hosted a cousins camp for my many nieces and nephews.

My daughters begged for a horse, but we couldn't afford to buy one.

One sunny Easter morning Dr. Sammi, one of Ray's flight students, drove up the lane in his truck and trailer. Ray grinned as he told the girls it was a surprise. The door opened and out stepped an old, kind, and gentle Belgian draft horse. Dr. Sammi's wife had rescued Oliver from slaughter. He was a New York City carriage horse. Immediately we changed his name to Goliath, which seemed a more appropriate fit due to his mammoth size. The girls were so happy to finally have a horse on the farm. They brushed and combed and braided his mane and tail. They rode him bareback as he slowly plodded along. I took many photos of Goliath and painted a picture of Bethany lying on his back. I titled the painting *Gentle Giant,* then later published it on many prints and cards.

Later, a bossy miniature horse named Maggie joined Goliath. He didn't mind that she was the boss.

I bought a brown-eyed jersey milk cow and named her Lizzie after my mother's mother. She provided the family with fresh milk, butter, and homemade ice cream. I learned how to culture buttermilk, sour cream, and yogurt. The children helped me care for Lizzie. I painted her portrait too and had the painting published. I simply titled it, *Lizzie.*

Today, many of our farm pets line the walls of my art gallery. Both of my daughters have kept their memories alive in stories they have written and published.

Josiah, my budding young artist, colored himself to sleep at night as a toddler. In the morning I had to fish the crayons out of the blankets and pillow-case. When he was thirteen, he began taking cartoon drawing classes held right here at the studio. When he was fifteen, his teacher took him on his first caricature gig. His first art job was drawing caricatures at a local amusement park. Later, I taught him how to do chalk talks. He helped me manage the many invitations that pour in daily. He later met his wife, who is also an artist, while doing caricatures at a wedding reception.

* My first art studio at Shady Lane Farm

* My daughter Bethany and her beloved Belgium, Goliath

CHAPTER 20

What's it Like to Be the Wife of a Pilot?

I AM OFTEN ASKED BY CURIOUS WIVES, "WHAT'S IT LIKE TO BE MARRIED TO A PILOT?"

I'd say adventurous, but of course like any career it's not without its challenges.

In the early years before I had children, I painted daily. With my art income, I helped with the costs of education as Ray continued in his quest to become a professional pilot. He trained evenings and weekends at Lancaster airport. Finally, the day came for his solo flight. I stood in the grass next to his flight instructor and watched the little Cessna take off, processing a number of feelings as I watched him disappear alone into the sky.

Ray quickly earned his instrument rating and multi-engine license, and then an instructor's rating. He then began to give evening flight lessons after his carpentry day job and on the weekends. I helped Ray advertise and organize airplane rides on Sunday afternoons, which finally began a financial return for his many costly years of training.

In 1999 he earned his Airline Transport Pilot Certificate. Immediately, a position as a copilot in a Learjet opened for him at Lancaster Airport with Venture Jets. Ray was very excited about his accomplishment.

And then his travels began.

"I'll need to go simulator training for a month in Wichita Kansas," he said, "then after that, a week trip in the Lear. What do you think?"

The realization hit me hard. At the time, we had three young children. I employed a niece to help keep up with the housework and to babysit on occasion. Still, I was left to feel like a well-supported single mom. Very often I was tempted to resent the unique challenges aviation caused our family. I watched other families sit together in the pew at church on Sunday mornings while our family sat without my husband. I realized this is what life was like for the wives of soldiers. I gained a new appreciation for their sacrifices for my freedom. I was determined to march out this challenge like a good soldier.

Ray experienced many adventures in his coast-to-coast travels. He enjoyed America's diverse scenery, visiting almost every state. But most of the time, travel for the life of the pilot is expressed in the saying: "Aviation is hours of boredom followed by moments of sheer terror."

"So what's the sheer terror part?" I asked naively.

"Oh, just the landings!" He said jokingly.

Oh dear, now I wasn't so sure I wanted to go along when the opportunity came for a flight to Colorado. I finally had the rare chance to travel with him. Ray ordered catering just for me, got me settled in my seat, then hopped into the captain's seat. I watched the scene out my window blur by as we raced down the runway. The force pushed my head back into the seat, and we soared through the clouds at five hundred miles per hour. Despite my initial anxieties I thoroughly enjoyed the experience. The landing was smooth, but not the sheer terror I had expected.

As Ray and I waited for the passengers to finish their business meetings, we visited the snowcapped Pikes Peak together. It was just as Katharine Lee Bates's song "America the Beautiful" described the scene. I saw amber waves of grain in the fields beyond the mountains. The color in the shadows of the clouds created the purple mountain majesties.

It was good for me to experience Ray's world. I presented him with a photo album of the pictures he collected from his travels. Unbeknownst to him, the album was a therapy that helped me to process the struggle I had with his job.

As lovely as the trip was, as it is in all my travels today, the best part of the trip is always to return home to the children and the farm.

September 2001 I got a call from one of Ray's students asking where Ray was.

"He's flying," I answered.

"Do you know where?" the caller asked.

"New York, I think. Why?" I asked.

After a long pause, he told me to turn on the television. Since we rarely watched TV, I first had to plug it in and attach the antenna. The reception was fuzzy at first, but then I saw the scene and heard the news that made me sick to my stomach. I waited for Ray's call as it was always his habit to call me right after landing. Finally, at 9:30 a.m., the phone rang. It was Ray.

"Oh, I'm so glad you're back. Did you hear what happened?" I asked.

"I sure did," he said somberly. He then described what he saw.

It was a beautiful clear morning at 6 a.m. when Ray left Lancaster Airport. Just as the sun was beginning to rise behind the majestic buildings of the New York City skyline on the return flight west, He flew directly towards New York City. Approaching the city at three thousand feet, He noticed smoke beginning to rise from the city. He figured it must be a fire, a very large fire, or a bomb explosion. Ray continued on the flight path that took him over the affected area. That's when He realized something bad had happened. That smoke was coming from one of the Twin Towers! From above, he could see a large gaping hole in the middle of the building. Still thinking it was a bomb, he watched blackened smoke cloud the clear morning sky. He watched debris fly from the hole and windows of the tower. Air traffic control radioed him asking if he could see the aircraft approaching the city with which they had lost contact. Ray looked but he was not able to spot the plane. He found out later it was, in fact, a plane that hit the second tower just as he was leaving the area. Again he received a call from ATC informing him that one or more aircraft had flown into the World Trade Center. All aircraft were diverted to the nearest airport, but Ray was allowed to continue and land at Lancaster airport. There he walked into the office and discovered, to his horror, that we were under terrorist attack.

I was relieved to have Ray back at the farm safe and sound. Together we continued to watch reports of additional attacks on the Pentagon and a third plane that did not complete its mission due to the heroic actions of passengers and crew who stormed the cockpit and overcame the hijackers. We watched and wondered what might happen next and grieved for innocent 911 victims.

I began adding images of the twin towers to my patriotic chalk talk pictures to remind us that freedom isn't free, but an earthly treasure to be actively cherished, protected, and preserved.

When I was close to expecting the arrival of our fourth child, Ray told me he had to leave for Oregon early the next morning. I expressed my concerns.

"Can't you get someone else to take the flight for you?" I asked.

"I tried but there was no one else available to take my place," He said. "Besides, the baby's not due for another two weeks; I'm sure I'll be back in time."

I went to the chicken house to talk to God. Having had several weeks of false labor, I prayed: "Lord, I believe it is your will that a father is present for the birth of his child. I'm going to trust you to arrange this birth." Then with authority, I spoke to the baby in my womb, "You will come at the proper time!" Then I returned to the house and refused to worry about it.

The next morning, 30 minutes before Ray was to leave for work, I went into labor. He called his boss. Now he had a legitimate reason to cancel the trip. Ray made arrangements for the other children. My dear friend Lisa Jorgensen, a certified nurse and midwife, arrived. We labored together.

Our fourth child, Jonathan David, which we nicknamed "Jon Boy" was born at home on November 11, 2003.

I had to learn not to focus on the constant disruptions and demands that charter flying put on the family schedule; causing plans to change often. I tried hard to keep life as consistent as possible for the children.

Many times over, I was thankful for the farm work to employ their little hands and minds. We made up many fun adventures that turned into the inspiration for their writing and art careers later in life.

* Our homestead from the bottom of the long stone lane

CHAPTER 21

Building Bridges with Art and Story

I OFTEN THOUGHT OF EDNA, THE MENNONITE ARTIST WHOSE WORK I LOVED AND ADORED.

I missed her as I had not seen her since the shunning. I wondered if she would see me if I stopped by her house. The chance came 20 years later when I was asked to entertain at a Mennonite retirement community's Christmas banquet close to Edna's house. As I neared her road, I wondered if she would receive my invitation to go with me. Was I too forward to ask? I decided it wouldn't hurt to try. I prepared myself for anything and knocked on the front door.

When she opened the door her face lit up. "Why Elva, it's you! Come in, come in!" She gushed.

"Oh I can't stay, I'm on my way to the Home to do a chalk talk and wondered if you might like to go along?" I asked.

"I saw you pictured in the newspaper and read about the chalk talks and I wondered what in the world it's all about!" She exclaimed excitedly.

"It's a really fascinating art, come with me and see," I urged.

"Oh, I'd love to, but I must first ask Moses." She scurried into the kitchen where her husband sat reading his Bible by lamplight. I stood in the doorway and listened as she asked, "Moses, it's Elva Hurst, she is on her way to do a chalk talk at the home, may I go along?"

He put his Bible down and looked at her over his reading glasses and answered, "I suppose so, if you aren't out too late."

I listened and realized I had almost forgotten that in the Old Order community, a wife was expected to ask her husband's permission before she did anything, almost as a child would ask a parent!

She skipped out the door with her big black bonnet in her hand and her black shawl flung over her shoulders. She jumped in my car and talked a mile a minute. It was just like old times; just as if the shunning had never happened.

It was a short but delightful time of catching up. After setting up my easel, I sat next to Edna and waited as a quartet played a lively Christmas carol with their fiddle, accordion, and harmonica. I looked over at Edna. Her face beamed brightly as she took in every note of the music. Her foot tapped in time with the tune. Then she leaned over and whispered loudly in my ear in her thick PA Dutch accent, "Ach, I chust don't understand why the bishop won't allow music, why, it's in the Bible all over the book of Psalms."

She thoroughly enjoyed the Christmas chalk talk I shared with the residents. When I dropped her off at her house, she thanked me over and over for taking her with me.

I went home and smiled as I wrote in my journal, "I think the shunning is over." The change that time and perspective brought to both of us was a sweet realization that art had reopened another door for me.

When I received an invitation to entertain the PA Holstein convention in Wilkes-Barre, PA, I considered what kind of program I could do for them. I wrote and developed a chalk talk titled *Farm Memories*. It included my thoughts on farm life and the inspirations that came from having had the privilege of being raised on a farm. I wanted it to include sound effects from the farm so I took my audio engineer to Dad's farm during milking time. We captured the sounds of the cows mooing, the cats meowing, and the general sounds of milking time.

Needless to say, my dad was curious. I told him that I would do the chalk talk at the next family gathering for Mom's birthday party in the fall.

Prior to that time, Dad would shun and show his disapproval by getting up and leaving the room whenever I began a chalk talk for the family at Christmas time.

On the day of our family gathering, Dad sat near the front. He enjoyed the chalk talk so much, he asked if I could do the chalk talk again so my oldest brother Paul could see it (he had arrived late after milking his herd of cows and missed the program). Before long, Dad became one of my biggest fans. When I visited, he'd ask about my chalk talk travels and helped me recall memories when writing *The Farm Life Series*, a collection of books about my childhood on the farm.

He offered details for the story of Billy, our pet raccoon my brothers found as a baby abandoned in the tree stump down in the meadow. They brought the frightened baby raccoon to the house where we feed him scrambled eggs and built him a treehouse home and called him Billy. We had many fun adventures with him. He always washed his food in his water dish before he ate it. Once we fed him mashed potatoes; we laughed as they dissolved in the water.

Dad told me one morning he was filling the tractor with fuel when he heard music coming from the barn. He went to investigate. In the milk house, he saw movement in the loose ceiling tiles. It was Billy turning the dials on the radio! Radios were forbidden in our home, but my brothers wanted a radio so badly that they bought one and hid it from Dad.

When the incident happened, I remembered Mom's quote from the Bible: "Be sure your sins will find you out."

My city friend heard me tell my farm pet stories in a chalk talk for children. "You should write those stories in a book!" she enthusiastically suggested.

"I'm not a writer," I told her.

"What do you mean you're not a writer? After all, you wrote the chalk talks!"

She planted a seed in my mind. I also noticed that when I shared with students in the public schools and asked how many lived on a farm, very few raised their hands. I realized I had many stories to tell. So I checked into the possibility of publishing a children's book. The cost nearly took my breath away. So I began to save money for printing. Finally, I published my first children's picture book in 2006 called *The Story of Woolly, My Pet Lamb*.

In 2008, I decided to write a chapter book for older children titled *The Pony Cart Adventure*. This book turned into a series called *The Farm Life Series* and was also adapted to film.

When Dad was in his mid-sixties, he suffered from a heart attack and needed bypass surgery. Before the operation, the hospital chaplain spoke with Dad concerning his salvation. Our pastor also visited with him and he reassured us that Dad had accepted Christ as his Savior and he was prepared for eternity. Dad recovered and returned home more peaceful and relaxed about life in his remaining years. He also came to recognize that his children, though no longer plain Mennonites, were still Christians, and he began to open his heart to us again.

My Dad passed away in August 2010, shortly after I published book four of The Farm Life Series called Then Comes Spring. I wrote a special note of thanks to Dad in the dedication and thanked him for the many farm life memories, many of which are scattered throughout the eight books of the series.

One day I got a surprise invitation from a minister in the church where I was excommunicated years earlier. He had heard about my chalk talks, and he was looking for some entertainment for his 50th wedding anniversary celebration. I set up the easel in the basement of his home and shared the farm memories chalk talk, which they as retired farmers enjoyed very much. I had a pleasant time catching up with many of my parents' acquaintances. I appreciated and respected how warm and receptive they were to me and my art even though I was no longer Mennonite. I was honored to spend such a pleasant evening with them.

Years later, my oldest sister got a surprise phone call from the bishop who excommunicated me and my siblings. They had a very pleasant conversation as he told her he had been reading the ministry materials that had influenced our change.

"I now understand," he said. "I'm sorry for what I did. Please tell your brothers and sisters that I'm sorry."

My sister had prayed for years that she would have the opportunity to speak with the bishop again before he passed on to glory. She hung up the phone and realized that her prayer had been answered.

In 2001, the local newspaper called for an interview. They wanted to feature an article about my chalk talks called "An Unlikely Artist." I agreed to meet with them. First, I met with the reporter and answered her many questions. She told me a photographer would be coming by to photograph the art in action. When he knocked on the door, I could tell something was wrong because he seemed very distracted. I had my easel and lights ready, he set up his camera, and I proceeded with my inspirational chalk talk. After a while, I heard sniffling sounds coming from behind. Unsure of what to do, I continued to draw. At the end of the chalk talk, I turned around to see tears streaming down his face.

"I'm so sorry," he apologized. "I don't know how to explain it, but something happened in my heart. Your story was just what I needed to hear, it touched my heart so much." Then his story spilled out...

Just that morning, his mother had been hospitalized with a mysterious illness and his wife of many years left him with no explanation. I reassured him of God's love and care for him in such a difficult time, then promised we would pray for him. The Bible says God's Words are Spirit and they are Life; they have the power to go beyond the surface and touch the deepest need of man.

I have a book at home which brings me much pleasure. I call it my "happy book"; a journal of sorts. It is full of stories just like this one about people whose lives were touched by the Word of God in the context of art. This is what motivates me to keep writing and creating more art.

In 2003 I began recording several of my programs on VHS with InFocus Productions. We also recorded an instructional chalk talk lesson, where I guided the viewers step by step through drawing a picture. I had my 8-year-old son, Josiah, follow along on a small easel as part of the "audience." In 2013 we commissioned Ben Mark Creative Productions to record several new chalk talks, as well as re-record DVDs of the old ones that were on VHS. With these products, people who came to see my performances were able to take this unique art of chalk talk home with them to share with others.

Several years down the road, I was contacted by a Korean news agency asking to come to my studio and interview me for their TV station while they were visiting Washington D.C. We arranged a date and time for them to come to my studio and record. They were particularly interested in my upbringing as a Mennonite and asked many questions about the local culture.

I was so grateful that the gospel was working not just through chalk talks locally but around the world through these recordings.

* Filming the introduction to a chalk talk DVD

CHAPTER 22

A Dream Realized

WHEN I BEGAN TEACHING ART LESSONS I HELD CLASSES IN OUR MUSTY, DIMLY LIT FARMHOUSE BASEMENT.

It was not a comfortable atmosphere, but I made do for 10 years. Then early one morning in 2008, I was returning from a prayer walk in the back fields, enjoying the sight of our bright red farm building coming into view among the treetops, when an idea came to mind; I could have an art studio in the back corner of the barn! With each step, the grand idea took shape. I would call it The Barnyard Art

Studio since it overlooks the barnyard and pasture. I started construction on it right away. Ray and the children all helped to clean out decades of old junk and tobacco lathe, as well as pigeon and mice dirt. We gathered up the beat-up car frames and tires left over from our neighbor boy's car repair adventures and sent them off to the junkyard. We scrubbed, stained, and varnished the ancient barn beams and nailed plywood on the walls, and put in large windows to provide plenty of natural daylight.

After some painting and decorating we opened for classes in the fall. To celebrate our grand opening, we held an open house event we called our Christmas Art and Craft Show. The local farming newspaper ran an article about an art studio in the barn which brought more students and visitors to the studio. I offered days of art on the farm for children in the summertime. We did hands-on art, realistic drawing, and plein air painting in the pasture. Then we'd stop for a picnic lunch and continue with more painting in pastels. For a special treat, I ended the day with a chalk talk. I told the students stories of artists gone before me. We were all inspired by the story of American artists Grant Wood and Grandma Moses.

As excited as I was to share these art adventures with students, I always had a sense the studio had even more potential.

Several years later I was asked to entertain the prestigious Officers' Wives Club in Fort Meade, MD.

After the chalk talk, I mingled with the ladies and chatted about their journeys and things they like to do off base. "Oh we love to shop in different towns," one lady exclaimed. "Do you have any ideas?"

"Have you ever visited the quaint town of Lititz up my way?" I asked them. Then I added, "If you'd like, you are welcome to come by my farm and visit my art studio, it is now open to the public."

They took me up on my offer. Several months later they called and said they were coming.

"Do you have room for a tour bus to turn around in your lane? We have 25 ladies and their husbands traveling with us. Do you have room for all 50? And oh, by the way, can we see another chalk talk while we are there?"

"Sure, come on by!" When I hung up the phone I realized what had just happened. Oh dear, how will I seat so many? I borrowed folding chairs from neighbors and friends.

When the large tour bus noisily made its way up the lane, the dog barked, the chickens ran out of the way, and the horses ran excitedly around the meadow.

Many of these ladies were from the city and some had never been in a barn before or seen an animal up close. They stood by the window taking pictures of the animals in the barnyard. They browsed the gallery and had a delightful time. After we said our goodbyes, I stood by the large studio window that overlooks the pasture and watched the bus go back out the lane. In my heart, I knew this is what I wanted to accomplish next with the studio.

The next day I checked the yellow pages for the contact information of tour companies nearby and sent a letter describing the chalk talk entertainment in the barn. The only one to respond was a shopping tour very interested in adding me to one of the stops on their tour. I agreed but that was not exactly what I had in mind. It wasn't until four years later that the pieces of my dream began to come together in a very unlikely way.

While I was entertaining with a chalk talk at an Eastern Star banquet, a tour operator from Brunswick Tours was in the audience. Sharon introduced herself to me and expressed how much she enjoyed the program. She told me later she went home trying to figure out a way to have her tour groups that visit Lancaster County experience a chalk talk.

Several months later, a bus group's itinerary included a shopping tour in nearby Lititz. Several days of non-stop rain forced the group to change their plans. Fran, the tour guide, called Sharon, asking, "What are we going to do with all this rain?"

"Well," replied Sharon, "what about Elva Hurst's barn?

Do you think she could do a chalk talk for us at her place?"

When they called to ask, I didn't hesitate to accommodate them. However, the heavy rain caused a roof leak in the old slate roof of the barn. I got two pots to catch the dripping water, then I set up my chalk talk easel and I set chairs around the studio so everyone stayed dry. The visitors were delighted to experience a chalk talk.

Another year passed when Sharon learned that Plain and Fancy Farms Restaurant was looking for on-site entertainment to complement their family-style dining for tour groups visiting Lancaster County. She recommended my performance art to the group coordinator and a meeting was held to discuss the possibility. They asked to see a chalk talk, so I shared with them my *Farm Memories* program. They were very impressed and decided to commission me to produce a chalk talk for them. After negotiations, I signed a contract to write, create, and produce the chalk talk. They wanted it to be titled *Faith and Forgiveness*. They wanted it to include my heritage and history and Ray's 9/11 story. They also wanted me to write about the tragic Amish school shooting. Mrs. Roberts, the shooter's mother, agreed to meet with me and kindly shared her heart and the facts about the incident. In the process, I made a new friend. She invited me to share with her support group. I also met with an Amish minister to be sure I did not misrepresent their life, culture, and response to the tragedy.

In 2013 the project was finished. Plain and Fancy promoted the chalk talk as an add-on feature for their dinner guests.

Meanwhile, at my art studio in the barn, tour group visits increased each year. It became apparent that it was time to expand. So, in the winter of 2014, we cleaned barn dirt and old hay out of the barn bay next to the art studio. We enclosed the open area, making a room large enough to accommodate more guests, creating a theater atmosphere with a stage for my chalk talk easel.

Thousands of chalk talks later, I still marvel at how effective this simple but meaningful art has been all these years.

While doing a chalk talk for a fundraiser for the care of orphans in a third-world country, I met up with the organizer of the event in the restroom while washing the chalk from my hands. I was surprised by her age. She looked to me to be quite elderly. I watched her as she applied some rouge to her cheeks. Then I told her I want to be like her when I "grow up."

"I want to be productive in my elderly years, I what to be doing chalk talks when I'm eighty," I said.

She paused then turned to me and grinned, "You'd better go for ninety," she urged.

"I'll take that!" I said. "I'll make that the goal of my faith."

I'm in my 31st year of chalk talks with public venues ranging from cruise ships to Amish schools and everything else in between. I've shared this art on a good many stages, but by far my favorite place to present is right here in my barn. So if you ever have the chance to visit Lancaster County, I hope you can join me in experiencing this delightful, old-time performance art. Meanwhile, I'll keep on drawing and collecting stories of lives touched by chalk, and thank God for the rich blessing it has brought to my life, and for the goodness of His mercy and the redemptive nature of his love.

* The studio entrance in the spring

OTHER PRODUCTS
BY ELVA & FAMILY

Visit elvaschalkart.com to order

The Pony Cart Adventure

"That's the thing about adventures, they never quite turn out the way you expect."

When eleven-year-old Elva finally finishes her chores on a beautiful summer morning, she hurries to the neighboring farm to see if her friend Linda can join her for an afternoon adventure. Come along with the young Mennonite girls as they hitch up the pony, climb into the cart, and trot down the lane for a day filled with unexpected excitement!

This charming film, based on the first book in the *Farm Life Series*, is the true story of Elva Hurst's growing-up years on the family farm. Reminiscent of days gone by, this film for families is full of good-hearted fun.

ORDER NOW!

Written and Illustrated
by Elva Hurst

A Collection of True Stories

These true stories recall my happy childhood days growing up in a large, loving Mennonite family. We lived in Lancaster County, Pennsylvania, in a community made up of many Amish and other Mennonite families who shared the big and small events of our lives.

Also available in audio CD

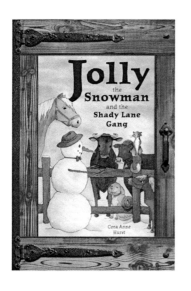

JOLLY THE SNOWMAN
AND THE SHADY LANE GANG

Every night, after the family has gone to bed, Jolly the snowman comes to life! He is introduced to a group of farm animal adventurers, who get into all kinds of mishaps as they explore the farm during the night.

A novel by Annie Hurst

INSPIRATIONS IN ART

A work of art is a reflection of the creative soul. Journey with Elva Hurst as she leads you through the sum and soul of her artistic inspirations.

A 9x11 coffee table book

MINI-BOOKS

These mini-books concisely cover the topics of fear, forgiveness in the midst of great wrong, and discovering how to walk in God's will through relationship with Him.

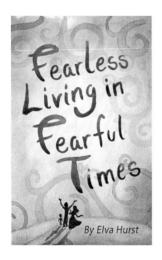

COME VISIT THE

BARNYARD ART STUDIO & GALLERY

ON THE BEAUTIFUL SHADY LANE FARM!

 Over 1200 sq. feet of multilevel, multiroom shopping

 Live chalk talk presentations by Elva available by appointment

 Homemade crafts and gifts, original art, antiques, and much more!

SEE WHERE THE INSPIRATION HAPPENS!

VISIT US ONLINE

to shop or schedule your visit!

WWW.ELVASCHALKART@GMAIL.COM
f ☺ BARNYARDARTSTUDIOGALLERY

JOHN 3:16

"For God so loved the world that He gave His only begotten
Son, that whoever believes in Him should not perish but
have everlasting life."